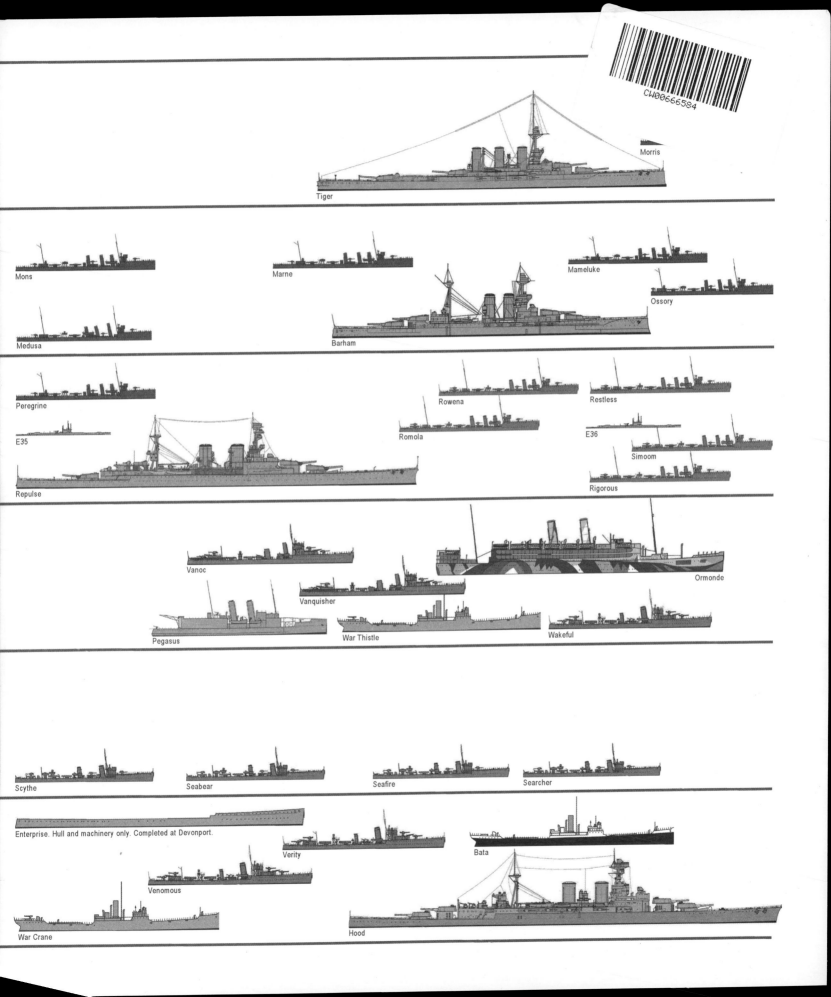

Morris

Tiger

Mons

Marne

Mameluke

Ossory

Medusa

Barham

Peregrine

Rowena

Restless

E35

Romola

E36

Simoom

Repulse

Rigorous

Vanoc

Ormonde

Vanquisher

Pegasus

War Thistle

Wakeful

Scythe

Seabear

Seafire

Searcher

Enterprise. Hull and machinery only. Completed at Devonport.

Verity

Bata

Venomous

War Crane

Hood

A SHIPYARD AT WAR

Unseen Photographs from John Brown's, Clydebank 1914-1918

IAN JOHNSTON

Seaforth
PUBLISHING

Title pages (overleaf): A view of the fitting-out basin on 8 July 1915. *Barham's* forward turrets, with guns installed and resting on trestles, await their roof plates. Painting the ship is underway, for which staging has been slung off the side of the hull. The three destroyers at the east quay are *Medusa* (outboard), *Mons* and *Marne* at the quay wall. (UCS1-118-GEN-283-2)

First published in Great Britain in 2014 by
Seaforth Publishing
An imprint of Pen & Sword Books Ltd
47 Church Street, Barnsley
S Yorkshire S70 2AS

www.seaforthpublishing.com
Email info@seaforthpublishing.com

British Library Cataloguing in Publication Data
A CIP data record for this book is available from the British Library

ISBN 978 1 84832 216 5

Typeset and designed by Stephen Dent
Printed and bound in China

CONTENTS

Acknowledgements 6

Sources 6

Introduction 7

Pre-war 16

1914 38

1915 60

1916 90

1917 124

1918 150

Post-war 176

Appendix 1: Shipyard diary 184

Appendix 2: Ships built or under construction 1914-1919 189

Index 191

ACKNOWLEDGEMENTS

This book would not have been possible without the support and co-operation of the National Records of Scotland and, in particular, Linda Ramsey, Head of Conservation and Eva Moya, Collections Conservator. Their appreciation of the importance of the Clydebank photographic collection and their determination to enable at least this small part of it to be brought to public attention on the anniversary of the First World War was of enormous assistance in making this work possible.

Thanks are also due to Ian Buxton, Brian Newman and Steve Dent for their expert comments and also to Paul Sweeney for reading the manuscript. I am grateful to David Hill for expert assistance in preparing captions for the internal views of *E35*. Grave danger awaits those who seek to interpret what photographs show from even such relatively recent times as the Great War, and, while I owe a great debt to the aforementioned, errors and misinterpretations are mine alone.

SOURCES

The Clydebank photographic archive, from which the images in this book are drawn, is held by the National Records of Scotland in Edinburgh and assigned the catalogue reference UCS1. UCS refers to the brief period from 1968 to 1972 when the Clydebank yard was part of ill-fated Upper Clyde Shipbuilders Ltd, which collapsed in June 1971.

The records of Clydebank shipyard that enabled the text and tables to be written are also held by the National Records of Scotland although housed by Glasgow University Archive Services in Glasgow. The main documents consulted were:

UCS1/1/1: Board Minutes
UCS1/10/2: Shipyard Diary

Additionally, Shipyard Managers Reports covering the 1914-18 period were consulted at Sheffield Archives where the records relating to the Sheffield-based activities of John Brown & Co Ltd are kept, although some Clydebank records are also held there. At the time of the author's visit, the few Clydebank documents that were there, including the Managers Monthly Reports, were uncatalogued.

INTRODUCTION

FOR A COUNTRY THAT ONCE DOMINATED THE SEAS, the photographs taken at John Brown's Clydebank shipyard during the First World War offer a remarkable insight into the ships and how they were constructed. This conflict was as much about industrial resources and capacity as it was about battle, and these images form one of the best records of industrial endeavour in the UK, and most certainly of the early years of twentieth-century shipbuilding. Although primarily concerned with recording ships under construction, the photographer's remit extended well beyond that to include a broader appreciation of the shipyard, its people and its setting. If more often identified with merchant vessels and magnificent ocean liners, Clydebank's output in the years prior to the First World War began to be populated with warships, reflecting British determination to stay ahead of Germany's growing naval presence. From August 1914 onwards, John Brown & Co would be a warship yard, building all types from the most iconic of capital ships to the diminutive destroyers and submarines. The completion of *Aquitania* for Cunard in May 1914 with its unrestrained opulence served to bring to a close an era to which there would be no return. The war years changed all that, and in the peace that followed the industrial, economic and social framework in which shipbuilding existed would never be quite the same again.

ABOUT THIS BOOK

My earlier book, *Clydebank Battlecruisers*, published in 2012, was based on photographs of British battlecruisers under construction between the years 1906 and 1920 at Clydebank. While there is a chronological overlap with this book, efforts have been made to ensure that no photograph has been duplicated of *Tiger*, *Repulse* and *Hood* and yet the story of the First World War could not be told without reference to these iconic vessels. The general intention has been to present the war years sequentially through the lens of the shipyard photographers at Clydebank.

It seems only appropriate that where the information is available, some reference should be made to the photographs and the people who took them. As far as I am aware, there is no photographic collection in the UK covering shipbuilding in the period from the 1880s to the early 1970s that is comparable with the collection made at Clydebank. It is true that other shipbuilders took photographs to record the progress of ships under construction, but these are more often concerned to record specific points such as launches, trials or notable events like lifting an engine on board. It seems that most shipbuilders hired the services of a local photographer rather than create in-house capability. Why management at Clydebank elected to incur the overhead of a resident photographic unit is not entirely clear.

What is evident in this collection, today and for future generations, is a clear and detailed study of how ships were built during the high period of British industrialisation, when more ships were built in this country than in any other, and when up to 250,000 people at peak times were so employed. That Clydebank shipyard should build many of the most important ships of the day, naval and mercantile, is more than good fortune and that the photographs should largely be of outstanding quality makes the collection exceptional.

ORIGINS OF CLYDEBANK SHIPYARD

Clydebank shipyard was established as one of the country's foremost builders of ships long before the outbreak of war in 1914. The company started in Glasgow in the middle of the nineteenth century when steam engineering was cutting-edge technology. A clutch of talented marine engineers established works by or near the River Clyde, spawning a great industry dedicated to the mechanical propulsion of ships reliably and efficiently. The engineers saw no barriers to building the ships to place their engines in and so shipbuilding came into being, an industry that would dominate and characterise the Clyde for decades to come.

The Thomson brothers, James and George, were engineers of that ilk and such was the success of their skill as designers and manufacturers of marine steam engines that they began shipbuilding at Govan in 1851. Twenty years later the business was transferred to a green-field site at what would become Clydebank. Here, a large shipyard was laid out, fortuitously opposite the confluence of the River Cart, providing ample launching space for the largest ships in an otherwise restricted River Clyde. Almost from the beginning, the Thomsons built large, fast and well-appointed ships for many shipping lines and most notably for Cunard.

By the end of the nineteenth century, Sheffield-based John Brown & Co Ltd had become one of the largest forge masters and manufacturers of armour plate in the UK. Following a pattern established by other armaments companies, and particularly Armstrong Whitworth & Co Ltd and Vickers Son & Maxim Ltd, John Brown added shipbuilding capacity to the business as a logical extension to their existing production. This select band of large firms were to find themselves well placed as Britain's response to German naval and mercantile ambitions accelerated. Added to that, and unforeseen before 1906, was the arrival of the 'revolutionary' battleship *Dreadnought*, which effectively obliged the Royal Navy to rebuild its battle fleet.

In 1899 the shipyard that John Brown & Co acquired was the Clydebank Shipbuilding and Engineering Co Ltd. John Brown was not the last armament company to diversify into shipbuilding, with Glasgow-based William Beardmore & Co doing the same in 1901 and Sheffield-based Charles Cammell in 1903, with the purchase of Laird's Birkenhead yard.

Although the Clydebank Works was already established in the front rank of shipbuilding, the new management brought with it experience, influence and expectation. Evidence of this was soon to follow in an impressive order book that included the prestigious Cunard liner *Lusitania* (launched 1906) and the battlecruiser *Inflexible* (1907). From the end of the 1890s, when war with Germany seemed a distant possibility given the passing of their Naval Laws, British shipbuilders benefited from a further expansion to the Navy, particularly after the introduction of the battleship *Dreadnought* in 1906, which rendered all existing battleships obsolete. The design and manufacture of heavy gun mountings in Britain at that time was dominated exclusively by Armstrong Whitworth at Elswick and Vickers Son & Maxim at Barrow. In 1907, to circumvent this duopoly, John Brown, in conjunction with Cammell Laird at Birkenhead and Fairfield at Govan, established the Coventry Ordnance Works to design and manufacture their own mountings. With existing works at Coventry and new works on the Clyde at Scotstoun, they acquired, with some difficulty, the necessary expertise to design and manufacture these complex mechanisms.

From then until the start of the First World War, John Brown's standing with the Admiralty was further developed with orders for the battle-cruisers *Australia* (1910), *Tiger* (1912) and the battleship *Barham* (1913), in addition to several destroyers and cruisers. From Cunard came the prestigious contract for the large North Atlantic liner *Aquitania* (1910).[1]

PHOTOGRAPHY AT CLYDEBANK SHIPYARD

For over one hundred years, ships great and small built at Clydebank shipyard were routinely photographed from keel laying to trials. Between the years 1899 and 1968, the shipyard was owned by John Brown & Co Ltd and it was during this period that many of the most significant ships built in Britain left the ways at Clydebank. However, it was not just famous ships that received photographic treatment, as all vessels from the late 1880s onwards were included.

Nearly thirty years before the First World War began and several decades after the dawn of industrial photography, the company then known as James & George Thomson & Co established a photographic unit at Clydebank shipyard to record ships under construction. This activity continued for over one hundred years and the photographs published here represent a small fraction of the collection.

'Progress of construction' photographs, as they were known, were taken by many shipyards to record and demonstrate progress over what could be a build time of several years, as well as for publicity purposes. The photographs generally followed a similar pattern, starting with an image of the keel on the building berth followed by general shots of the hull on the berth with details such as a stern frame or shaft brackets. Launching was covered with a series of shots, while fitting-out included overall and detail shots showing machinery and gun mountings and various superstructure elements being added until completion. Departure from the yard and trial views completed the series. Sensitivity surrounding warship contracts, as well as the Official Secrets Act, did not restrict photography, although very few shots were taken internally of completed warships: of over 500 photographs taken of *Hood*, for example, none were taken of her interiors.

Work in the shops, where the steel components and sub-assemblies were fashioned, was not usually covered, although completed machinery, turbines, boilers and condensers, etc, were often photographed where they were manufactured. Periodically, the photographers would take general shots of the yard or of groups of people like the John Brown Choir and, from time to time, record images of ships built elsewhere on the Clyde passing by the yard. Inevitably, the presence of an in-house photography department resulted in the occasional passport photo for senior management.

While photographing ships under construction was nothing new, what appears to set Clydebank apart is the scale of the operation. From the company's records, the first mention of photographers is on 29 June 1887, when two men are recorded in the wages books under the heading of photography: J Stuart, paid £6 fortnightly, and D Wallace, presumably an assistant or apprentice, paid ten shillings fortnightly. The employment of photographers at this date coincides with the company winning the prestigious orders for the Inman liners *City of New York* and *City of Paris*, then among the largest liners to be built. As an adjunct of the developing shipbuilding and marine engineering business at Clydebank, photography grew and by April 1904 five persons were entered into the wages book under photography:

D Lindsay, £4 10s per week
T Berry, £2 6s
P Forbes, £2
W McCreadie, £1 8s
J Butters, £1.

This suggests a senior photographer, a photographer and three assistants. In November 1919 nine people are on the books, with Lindsay receiving £5 15s 6d and Berry £3 15s 6d per week. None of the others earned over £1 5s per week. From this it seems certain that the photographs reproduced in *Clydebank Battlecruisers* and in this book were taken by D Lindsay and T Berry, and to them and the management of the day due acknowledgement must be made for such a fine record of these fascinating ships. At the height of the depression in May 1932, when work on the Cunarder *Queen Mary* had been suspended and only a few hundred men remained in the yard, Lindsay and Berry were still on the books at £5 1s and £2 14s 6d respectively.

The very first images taken at Clydebank were recorded onto glass plates, 12x10 inches in size although 15x12 and 10x8 plates were used frequently. Large plate cameras continued to be used until after the Second World War when half-plate and 5x4 celluloid negatives, and later two and a quarter square, come into use.

The first warship to be systematically photographed, albeit sparingly, was the battleship *Ramillies*, launched in 1892. According to a list of photographs kept by the shipyard, the following images were captured of the ship: ten of a model, some of which depicted a working model; two of the hull on the stocks, four of her launch, seventeen of deck details, four showing panels in the admiral's cabin, two showing the electric turning gear in the barbette and eight of the ship on trials.

However, subsequent coverage of warships produced more images, although mostly exterior shots, as shown by this selection from the catalogue:

Barham, battleship, 281
Repulse, battlecruiser, 359
Hood, battlecruiser, 502
Australia, cruiser, 229
Fortune, destroyer, 45
Southampton, cruiser, 104
Duke of York, battleship, over 600
Indefatigable, fleet carrier, 441
Bermuda, cruiser, 209
Barrosa, destroyer, 119.

Passenger vessels, where internal views were taken as a matter of course, fared better in overall numbers:

Lusitania, 76
Queen Mary, 1016
Caronia, 1131
Carinthia, 650
QE2, over 4000.

When the last ship left Clydebank in 1972 following the collapse of Upper Clyde Shipbuilders, of which John Brown & Co had become the Clydebank Division, the records of the Clydebank company including the photographs were saved for the nation. There are 23,000 glass plate negatives and at least another 20,000 celluloid negatives plus an additional number of uncatalogued celluloid and small glass plate negatives. While the photographs provided a record of construction and the occasional publicity shot, one immediate product was the creation of bound volumes, often several for a significant vessel, containing contact prints from the glass plate negatives. Today, the negatives and bound volumes are under the care of the National Records of Scotland in Edinburgh who are conserving, recataloguing and scanning the collection for posterity.

While it is likely that the attention given to photography at Clydebank was out of the ordinary, it is nevertheless sad to note that the photographic collections of other well known shipbuilders such as Palmers, Fairfield and Armstrongs, as well as many smaller companies, have not fared as well and in some cases barely exist at all. Much of this loss can be attributed to the casual disposal when firms closed of company records that had previously been carefully maintained over the years – tales abound of glass plate negatives and other important documents dumped in skips or thrown on bonfires. This makes the photographic collection of Clydebank shipyard all the more significant.

THE FIRST WORLD WAR AT CLYDEBANK

On the eve of war John Brown & Co Ltd fully expected to play its part in the conflict by progressing urgently required warships as quickly as possible. There were many uncertainties, however, and questions that had no immediate answers. If the war was prolonged, major disruption to seagoing commerce was certain, with consequences for the mercantile trade and the building of merchant ships with which John Brown was established and reliant upon as a cornerstone of its business. If the war was of short duration, and there was a feeling among some that it would be over by Christmas, then the interruption to normal business would be minimal.

When the realisation dawned that the war would not be over by Christmas, coupled to the reality of the war at sea, new and urgent requirements began to affect the types and numbers of ships planned. An early move was away from battleships and the headlines generated by the numbers built which had so characterised the years up to 1914, as it was clear in any case that Britain was winning that particular battle. Serious deficiencies in the number of destroyers, submarines and certain classes of cruisers emerged, but all of this was to some extent overshadowed by the crippling and potentially disastrous merchant ship losses, which came to a head in 1917. These deficiencies and losses had to be made good by a shipbuilding industry already working close to maximum capacity. The longer the war lasted, the more it would place demands on industrial output and closer inspection of how this was achieved. As the scale of these requirements emerged, it became necessary to put in place some form of tighter, more efficient, control of shipbuilding, as for all war-related manufacturing, in order to maximise output and intercede in the supply and direction of skilled manpower, arguably one of the most vital constraints of the war effort. The means chosen by the War Cabinet was the passing of the Munitions of War Act in July 1915, which in the case of ship construction gave the Admiralty wide powers to provide a strategic overview of the shipbuilding industry. Under this Act, factories, shipyards and other industrial concerns deemed essential to the war effort

were declared Controlled Establishments. Senior Admiralty appointments were made in each of the shipbuilding districts which monitored the activities of individual yards, with the ability to switch labour from one to the other or to reprioritise the labour attached to a particular type of ship where such vessels were not deemed important. The same applied to ships and even individual machinery contracts themselves or, more particularly, to the resources required to complete them. If spare capacity existed at one yard, where another yard was overstretched, the contract would be switched if it was practically possible. This happened on several occasions at Clydebank, when engine contracts were given to John Brown's where spare capacity existed, and also with heavy crane capacity, such as in the fitting of large calibre ordnance and mountings in monitors. In the rapid construction of *Renown* and *Repulse,* labour was repeatedly redirected around and the battleship *Ramillies*, on the stocks at Beardmore's Dalmuir yard, was denuded of steelworkers in an effort to accelerate *Renown*. Providing manpower for the armed services militated against ramping up manufacturing output and a partial solution to this was found in introducing women to the shipyards and engine shops, previously unthinkable in those days.

All of these measures cut across established commercial and working practices, as well as long fought for trade union rights, but were deemed admissible, if not essential, given the national emergency. These moves to mobilise all of the nation's resources took hold late in 1914, by which time there was stalemate on the Western Front and a war of attrition underway.

THE WORKS

The Clydebank Works were large by the standards of the day, extending over 80 acres and comprising two separate yards, East and West, divided by a fitting-out basin where hulls were taken after launch for completion. There were five large building slips in the East Yard, the smallest of which could accommodate vessels from 600 up to 900 feet in length. The West Yard had four shorter building slips, although it was possible to build several small ships on all berths should the circumstances require it. The yard was equipped with numerous lattice derrick cranes of 5 tons capacity on each slipway, two covered berths and two large fitting-out cranes, each capable of lifting 150 tons.

The Clydebank Works also included extensive engine and boiler shops where the machinery was constructed for all of the ships built there, as well as for ships building elsewhere. The Company played an historically significant role by installing Parsons turbines in the first turbine-powered liner *Carmania* in 1905, after first building an experimental turbine in 1904. Moreover, John Brown had become the sole UK developer and licensee of the Curtis turbine developed by Charles Curtis at the Schenectady works of General Electric in the United States. For a time before, during and after the First World War, this turbine found favour with the Admiralty alongside the Parsons type and often in preference to the latter.

Whether by design or accident, Brown's output of capital ships was dominated by battlecruisers, of which no fewer than five were built, from *Inflexible* (1907) to *Hood* (1918).[2] Clydebank's only battleship of the period, *Barham*, thought of as a fast battleship, lends weight to the view that Clydebank's expertise in constructing high-power turbine machinery, not least their own Brown-Curtis type from 1911 onwards, was a factor in this run of contracts.

Maintaining workflow through such a complex industrial operation as a large shipyard, with so many separate processes running concurrently, was a significant organisational achievement. Output from the shipyard was determined by a number of factors which could be equated, in simplistic terms, to the number of building slips available, coupled to the productive capacity of the steel-working shops and the labour applied to it. With those assets, management effort was focused on maximising the amount of material that could be delivered and erected on the building ways – what later came to be known as productivity. Given a constant supply of orders, the worst that could happen was an insufficiency of skilled labour. In the modern history of shipbuilding, apart from trade fluctuations, labour was the most volatile element, either through the lack of it, as evidenced in both world wars, or through poor industrial relations – the blunt interaction between labour and employers regarding working conditions and practices – and manifest, at worst, in the use of the strike by the workforce or the lockout by management.

Throughout the First World War employment at John Brown's was maintained at an average of 10,000 workers, split typically between the shipyard (7000) and the engine works (3000). Up until a ship was launched, the majority of labour required was drawn from the steel trades, or 'ironworkers' as they were popularly referred to at the time, a hangover from the iron era of 1840 to 1880.[3] After launching, the balance of trades shifted from the steel trades to the fitting-out trades: plumbers, electricians, joiners and numerous subcontractors. When order books were full, steelworkers and fitting-out trades were rotated from one contract to maintain continuity of construction and steel throughput. When order books were thin or if a gap in production was unavoidable, men were dismissed and often in great numbers.

The construction time for *Tiger*, most of which took place during peacetime, was 75.5 weeks from keel laying to launch and 38 weeks from fitting-out until completion,[4] a total of 28.3 months. The departure of this ship was accompanied by the dismissal of 2000 men over a two-month period because of a gap in production. Of the 2000, approximately 1000 were from the shipyard and the remainder from the engine works. Once returned to the job market, they would have been quickly employed in other yards and engine works, on the Clyde or elsewhere. This relationship based on the hiring and firing of labour was nothing new and presented itself habitually to shipbuilders trying to balance employment and the retention of key skills with contracts at different stages in the construction cycle, and always with profit in mind.

Employing the right number of men was crucial in terms of fulfilling contract conditions and thus achieving the expected profit levels. Getting the balance right demanded fine judgement. In January 1914 Thomas Bell,[5] John Brown's Works Manager at the Clydebank Works, lamented the difficulties found in employing additional ironworkers for his burgeoning order book. The Company could employ and retain between 2400 and 2500 ironworkers alone but needed a further 300 to keep, as Bell noted, 'on the right side of the line with our shipyard charges and come nearer to Government delivery requirements.'[6]

If this then was the way in which shipyard labour ebbed and flowed during peacetime, during the war, the labour situation rapidly crystallised. Firstly, for yards like John Brown's, there was an apparently endless supply of naval work and a diminishing supply of labour given the call to arms. During the 1914–1918 period, 2350 employees from the works joined the armed forces, representing one quarter of the workforce.[7] Secondly, the bulk of the work demanded men of the steel trades, as warships required fewer fitting-out trades, such as carpenters, plumbers and electricians, than a cargo or passenger ship. Thus platers, riveters and the others associated with the steel trades, like caulkers and drillers, were

at a premium. Thirdly, the open market that was normally capable of regulating the supply of men from one yard to another could not operate, because yards had no foreseeable need to let men go, such was the volume of Admiralty orders on hand. As yards moved closer to achieving maximum output with high levels of manpower, the labour market effectively ceased to exist. On 12 July 1915 the Ministry of Munitions informed the management of John Brown & Co that the company was now a Controlled Establishment, which meant that labour would be allocated to contracts according to a priority system.

Faced with the somewhat contradictory demands of sending men to the front while at the same time maintaining high output in the factories and shipyards at home, a further measure was introduced in the form of 'dilution'. This scheme relied essentially on drafting women into industry to take over labouring, and semi-skilled work where possible. While such measures would normally have been unacceptable by the standards of the day, let alone to the unions, the situation was desperate enough for agreement to be reached, provided that the women gave up their jobs once hostilities had ended. By August 1916 dilution had been established in 150 of the largest 300 controlled engineering and shipbuilding establishments on Clydeside alone. It was claimed that this involved 14,000 women.[8] In November 1916 Thomas Bell stated:

> The Admiralty most seriously continue to impress on us the importance of dilution and of employing as many women as possible. Whilst we have been able to effect considerable dilution in the manning of smaller machines in the Engine Shops and in deploying clerks in the Counting House, it has not been easy to effect dilution in the shipyard. [We] have started [women] in the Joiners Shop and hope to have several women in the Plumbers Shop, Sheet Iron Shop and Sawmill.[9]

By 8 January 1918 the number of persons employed in John Brown's shipyard, not including the engine works, was 5270 of whom only 87 were women.[10]

A further threat to employment levels materialised in December 1916 when the Ministry of Munitions sought to remove immunity from call-up from semi-skilled and unskilled workers. This immunity, in the form of War Service Badges or Certificates, had been awarded to workers in recognition that shipbuilding was essential war work. Employers were now requested to 'de-badge' their workers and enter their names on a list to be returned to the Ministry of Munitions, thus enabling the Ministry to call them up. Men sent to the front would be replaced by substitutes, 'men of military age not required for service with the Colours or such other men and women as may be available'. The scheme drew a quick response from the Employer's Federation, which emphasised the serious effect on production that the removal of these men would have. It was subsequently agreed that semi-skilled and unskilled shipyard workers would not be called up without the prior agreement of the Admiralty.[11] While employment figures dropped after this was introduced, so many factors influenced employment levels that it is not clear whether it was solely attributable to this measure.

At Clydebank in April 1915 Thomas Bell introduced pneumatic riveting to the shipyard in an attempt to make more efficient use of labour. A pneumatic riveting gun required only one man to operate it at the face of the plate (there would be a man behind the plate, a 'holder-on' to hold the rivet in place), enabling one riveter to close a rivet where previously

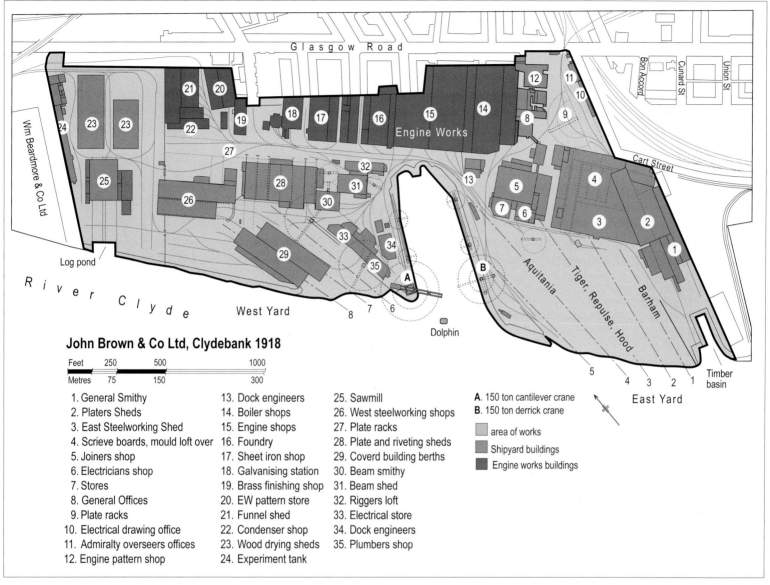

John Brown & Co Ltd, Clydebank 1918

Feet 250 500 1000
Metres 75 150 300

1. General Smithy
2. Platers Sheds
3. East Steelworking Shed
4. Scrieve boards, mould loft over
5. Joiners shop
6. Electricians shop
7. Stores
8. General Offices
9. Plate racks
10. Electrical drawing office
11. Admiralty overseers offices
12. Engine pattern shop
13. Dock engineers
14. Boiler shops
15. Engine shops
16. Foundry
17. Sheet iron shop
18. Galvanising station
19. Brass finishing shop
20. EW pattern store
21. Funnel shed
22. Condenser shop
23. Wood drying sheds
24. Experiment tank
25. Sawmill
26. West steelworking shops
27. Plate racks
28. Plate and riveting sheds
29. Coverd building berths
30. Beam smithy
31. Beam shed
32. Riggers loft
33. Electrical store
34. Dock engineers
35. Plumbers shop

A. 150 ton cantilever crane
B. 150 ton derrick crane

area of works
Shipyard buildings
Engine works buildings

two riveters, each using a hammer, were required. However, because of the reluctance of the riveters to use pneumatic tools, Thomas Bell brought forty squads of pneumatic riveters to Clydebank from Swindon and also from northwest England. The inducement for this was found in building new homes for the incomers. As the bulk of riveting carried out in the yard was still done by hand and hammer, a similar inducement was offered to local riveters to encourage them to take up the pneumatic riveting tool.

The introduction of new facilities and tools played a part in raising output. By the financial year-end, 31 March 1916, £57,200 had been spent on improvements to the yard.[12] In January 1918, further enhancements to the West Yard totalling £50,000 were applied for under Admiralty Extension No 130. This expenditure was expected to secure a 30 per cent increase in output from both West Yard berths.

Overall numbers employed at Clydebank averaged about 10,000 persons. At the beginning of September 1914 10,535 people were in employment in the shipyard and engine works. This fell to a low of 8017 at the beginning of March 1915 and reached a peak of 10,895 at the beginning of June 1915.

This then was the background to the naval shipbuilding programme that got underway in earnest in the late summer of 1914.

THE SHIPBUILDING PROGRAMME 1914–1918

In broad terms, the shipbuilding programme of 1914–1918 was dominated by three classes of ship: capital ships, destroyers and, to a lesser extent, standard merchant ships. When war was declared, two capital ships were under construction, *Tiger* and *Barham*, both of which might be described as the last of the legacy ships, being part of the enormous rebuilding of the battle fleet that had begun in 1906 with *Dreadnought*. With the battleships of the *Queen Elizabeth* and *Royal Sovereign* classes due to complete in 1915, it was clear that the Grand Fleet would far outweigh the High Seas Fleet in the number of battleships deployed or soon to be deployed. New developments and altered circumstances changed that complacency. The success of the battlecruisers in the first naval engagements in which that new type of ship was involved, coupled to the return of its progenitor, Lord Fisher, as First Sea Lord, prompted the building of two new vessels of that type, carrying the heaviest guns

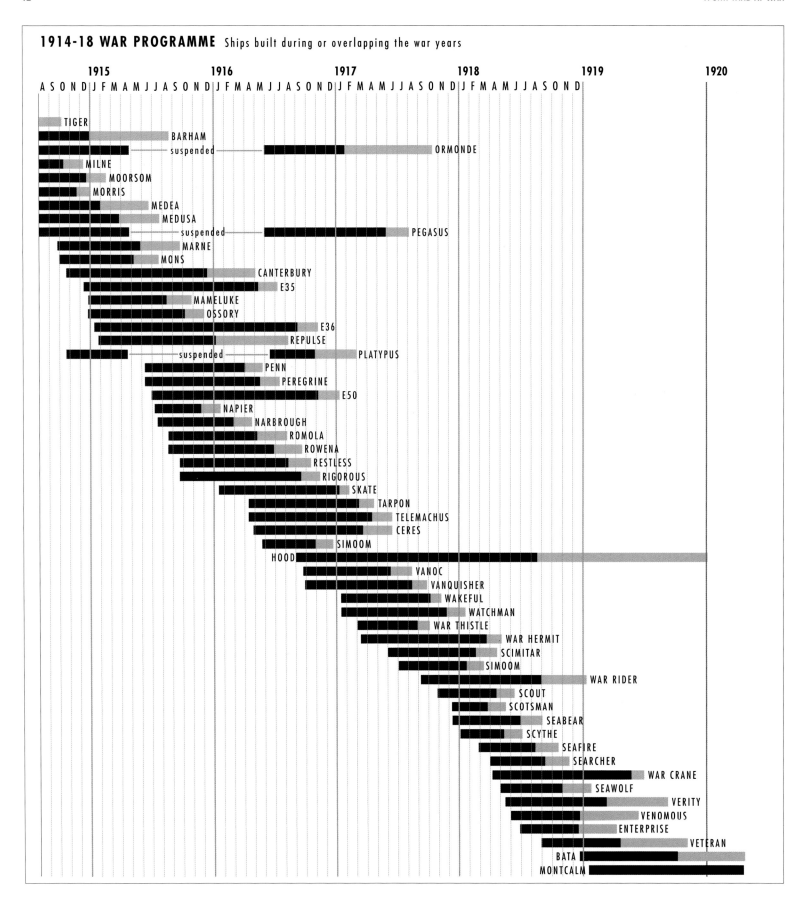

1914-18 WAR PROGRAMME Ships built during or overlapping the war years

on hulls capable of the fastest speeds then achieved by capital ships. Like the ships themselves, everything about the origin and construction history of these vessels, *Renown* and *Repulse*, happened at high speed. Initially ordered as *Royal Sovereign* class battleships from Fairfield's and Palmer's, at Fisher's behest in December 1914 they were changed to battlecruisers. This followed the spectacular conclusion to the Battle of the Falkland Islands where the British battlecruisers *Invincible* and *Inflexible* had hunted down and sunk Admiral Von Spee's squadron. From the Director of Naval Construction's offices to the shipbuilders concerned, things moved at a feverish pace to design the ships, prepare building berths and reassign materials already ordered for the battleships and begin ordering new equipment for the battlecruisers. The DNC first became aware of the project on 19 December and the shipbuilders at the end of that month.

It immediately became apparent that Palmer's shipyard did not have the physical space to accommodate the extra length of their ship, *Repulse*, and the order, along with the building material already assembled at Jarrow, was transferred to John Brown's at Clydebank. With Fisher's customary zeal, everything had to happen at breakneck speed and on 25 January, barely five weeks after the DNC first heard of them, the keels for both ships were laid down. The subsequent construction history of *Renown* and *Repulse* broke all records for ships of their size, resulting in build times of just 20 and 19 months respectively.

The other capital ship begun at Clydebank during the First World War was the battlecruiser *Hood*, the design of which was finalised in April 1916 with orders for four ships of the type placed on the 19th of that month. Designed to counter German battlecruisers, the construction of the *Hood* class was immediately frustrated by the catastrophic consequences of the Battle of Jutland on 31 May in which three British battlecruisers were sunk. Ruminations and reflections on the design of British battlecruisers gripped the DNC's department as the scheme of armour of the *Hood* class was reworked, resulting in a net addition of over 5000 tons to the original design. *Hood* was laid down on 1 September, probably to the original design, while details of the revised version were fed into the design and construction process. This resulted in slow progress on the building slip as information filtered through to the shipbuilder well into 1917. The Admiralty never really pushed *Hood's* construction, although completion in December 1918 was a possibility. Insufficient labour and competing demands for what was available played a part in a slow rate of building, as did the late supply of her main armament mountings from Vickers at Barrow.

The construction of submarines had been largely concentrated at two locations, Vickers at Barrow and HM Dockyard, Chatham. Before the war, the Admiralty sought to increase the supply of submarines and encouraged other shipbuilders, including John Brown, to become active in this field. The first submarine, *E35*, was laid down in November 1914, although Brown's experience with this vessel was not a good one, after a launching incident where the boat fell off the launching ways during the initial stages of her launching run. In the event, only three submarines were constructed at Clydebank. By far the most numerous class of warship built by John Brown and many other shipbuilders was the destroyer, following the realisation that there were insufficient destroyers to screen the battleships and battlecruisers of the Grand Fleet. At Clydebank, a total of 42 destroyers were ordered throughout the conflict, all of which were delivered, with the exception of five Modified W class ships cancelled at the end of 1918.

THE DESTROYER PROGRAMME 1914–1918

More destroyers were built at Clydebank than at any other single location in the UK during the war. Analysis of the times taken to construct these small vessels does show improvements on successive build times, but not as consistently as might have been expected, and certainly not in comparison to modern standards. Although detailed operational considerations, which may never be known at this distance, undoubtedly played a role in this, two obvious factors militated against constant improvement in build times – the drip-feed nature of the ordering process and the change in design seen through different classes of ship. While all of this is understandable given the need to respond flexibly to changing circumstances at sea, it made the shipbuilder's task in expediting orders more difficult. During the first year of the war, the run of M class and Repeat M class destroyers (always referred to more accurately at the time as Torpedo Boat Destroyers), showed a general reduction in build times, resulting in *Napier* taking just 201 days in comparison to *Moorsom*, which required 356 at the beginning of the programme, although the fitting-out period was similar for both. Inexplicably, after *Napier* the numbers rise for the last three of the Repeat Ms, although this may have been due to *Repulse*, which served as a manpower magnet throughout its brief construction period at Clydebank. It is difficult to explain why R class *Simoom* notched up 214 days while the rest of the class took a minimum of 350 days, although *Tarpon* and *Telemachus* were fitted as minelayers. Of the two ships built for both the V and W classes, surprisingly, the second took longer than the first. With the smaller S class there was more consistency to build times and another construction record in building *Scotsman*. In April 1918 the Controller wrote to the Company acknowledging its achievements in building the destroyer *Sesame* in 7.5 months and setting a record for the fastest build time of any ship of this class:

> [I] invite attention to the satisfactory performances of Messrs. John Brown & Co. Ltd. in the matter of time taken by them to build destroyers. This Firm, have since the outbreak of war, delivered 25 Admiralty destroyers and 2 originally intended for the Greek Government, a larger number than any other firm in the country. They made the first deliveries of the vessels of the V and W classes, ordered in July/16 and Dec/16 respectively, and have already delivered 2 of the S class, ordered April/17, viz. *Simoom* and *Scimitar*, no other firm having yet delivered a destroyer of that date of order. *Simoom* was laid down 6/8/17 and delivered 12/3/18 i.e. a building period of 7 months…[14]

A few months after this letter was received, John Brown beat their own record, building the S class destroyer *Scotsman* in under 6 months (163 days) from keel laying to departure and *Scythe* in 6.5 months (187 days).[15] The three Modified Ws, although laid down during the last months of the war, were not subject to wartime conditions and fitted out at a more leisurely rate. Five other Modified Ws (*Vigo*, *Wistful*, *Virulent*, *Volage* and *Volcano*) were ordered in 1918 and all cancelled at the war's end. Of these it is likely that work had begun on at least two.

By the spring of 1917 the loss of merchant ships to U-boats was running at a critical level, following the resumption of unrestricted submarine warfare. Replacing merchantmen became top priority and even in yards almost exclusively devoted to warship construction like John Brown's, any capacity that became available was seized upon. The Controller of Merchant Shipping placed an order for two Standard ships,

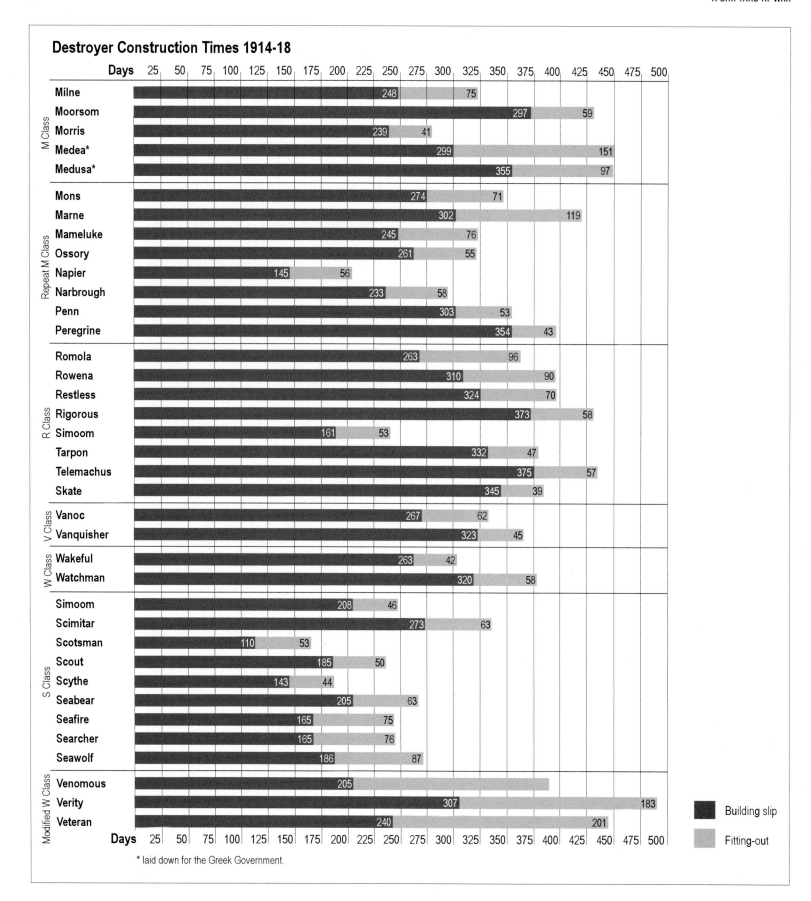

Destroyer Construction Times 1914-18

War Thistle and *War Hermit* laid down in March, followed by two others, *War Rider* and *War Crane* in September 1917 and April 1918. A fifth ship was laid down in December 1918 and completed as *Bata* for Elder Dempster in October 1919.

The Orient liner *Ormonde* and the ferry *Stockholm* for the Great Eastern Railway Co were under construction when war broke out. Initially, labour was removed from both vessels and directed to warships that were required urgently, *Tiger* and then *Barham*. Both contracts were suspended in April 1915 and not restarted until a need arose for them. Subsequently, with minimal alteration, *Ormonde* was completed as a troopship in October 1917, while *Stockholm* was redesigned as a hybrid seaplane and aircraft carrier, renamed *Pegasus* and completed in August of the same year.

In October 1918, with the end of hostilities imminent, the Admiralty wrote to John Brown & Co stating their intention to decelerate some warship work in favour of merchant work. They ranked the effort to be applied to warships in order of importance from one (most rapid) to three (least rapid) as follows:

Hood, Enterprise, Seafire, Searcher and *Seawolf*
Sesame, Venom, Verity, Veteran and *Vigo*
Wistful and *Virulent*.

The letter stressed: 'It is essential there should be no delay in the delivery of *Hood, Enterprise, Seafire, Searcher* and *Seawolf*. Delivery of the remaining vessels may be extended to give deliveries by April 1920.' It also advised that work on *Volage* and *Volcano* should stop immediately and that the contracts might be cancelled altogether.[16] In the event, the contracts for *Vigo, Wistful, Virulent, Volage* and *Volcano* were cancelled. The fitting-out of *Hood* was delayed when it became clear that the 15-inch gun mountings would not be delivered until late 1919. In any case, following the end of hostilities in November 1918, the pressure was off and she ended up taking 16 months to fit out, almost the same time it had taken to build *Repulse* from the keel up. *Hood* left Clydebank to begin a first series of trials on 8 January 1920.

The end of the war brought with it an abrupt end to naval orders for which shipbuilders had been well prepared by the Admiralty. On 10 January 1919 what might be termed normal work resumed at Clydebank with the keel laying of the intermediate liner *Montcalm* for Canadian Pacific Railways. This was followed later in the year by two ferries for Great Eastern Railway Co, *Antwerp* and *Bruges*, the liner *Franconia* for Cunard and *Montclare*, a sister ship to *Montcalm*. Last of the War Programme ships, *Hood* remained until January 1920 and with her departure Clydebank shipyard was once more returned to the realm of merchant shipbuilding. With an abundance of orders the prospects looked good – or so it seemed. The 1920s would be nothing like as good as the pre-war years.

OUTPUT 1914–1918

Statistics published in December 1918[17] listed 47 ships built during the war period, totalling 155,153 displacement tons and 1,563,500 indicated horsepower.[18] These figures excluded *Hood*, even though she had been launched and her machinery constructed by the end of the war. John Brown's own figures stated output as 205,430 tons and 1,720,000 HP.[19]

In addition to constructing the machinery of the ships listed in the accompanying table, the engine works turned out machinery for vessels under construction at other yards as follows:

- two sets of machinery for K class submarines *K1* and *K2*
- machinery for the battleship *Canada*
- machinery for the Russian battleship *Imperator Aleksandr III*
- machinery for the Chilean battleship *Almirante Cochrane* (later the carrier *Eagle*)
- three sets of machinery for destroyers *Noble, Nomad* and *Sesame*
- one half-set of machinery for the battlecruiser *Furious*
- sixteen watertube boilers for eight patrol vessels and two sets of turbines for two of them
- machinery for one cargo steamer
- five sets of boilers for standard vessels
- three sets of boilers for rescue tugs.[20]

NOTES

1 Despite the focus on large vessels given here, Clydebank was equally concerned with the building of smaller vessels including cruisers, destroyers, cargo vessels and paddle steamers.

2 This run of battlecruiser orders was continued into the 1920s with the award of the contract to build one of the G3 battlecruisers, although the vessels were subsequently cancelled.

3 Although the use of steel was widespread from the 1880s onwards, men of the steel trades were often referred to as ironworkers and the shops they worked in as the ironworking sheds.

4 Completion in this instance is taken as the date on which *Tiger* left the yard.

5 In May 1917 Thomas Bell left John Brown & Co temporarily to serve as Deputy Controller of Dockyards and War Shipbuilding. He returned to Clydebank in January 1919 and was knighted in 1918.

6 UCS 1/5/13, Thomas Bell's memo on the shortage of ironworkers, 26 January 1914.

7 *Glasgow Herald Trade Review*, 28 December 1918. Of the 2350 who enlisted, 101 were killed in action and many more incapacitated.

8 *Lennox Herald*, 30 August 1916.

9 Uncatalogued Managers Monthly reports for 2 November 1916, held at Sheffield Archives, Sheffield.

10 UCS 1/22/5. Plant Files. Papers concerning Admiralty Extension 130, a scheme of improvements at Clydebank Shipyard.

11 UCS1/21/32. This file contains the printed letter to employers from the Ministry of Munitions announcing the scheme, accompanied by forms to be completed by employers listing the 'de-badged' men. The overall effect of this scheme appears to have been blunted, at least in the shipbuilding industry, by the response made by the Shipbuilding Employers' Federation.

12 UCS 1/22/4. Plant Files. Letter from the Ministry of Munitions dated 20 June 1916.

13. UCS1/22/5. Plant Files. Papers concerning Admiralty Extension 130. The Company expected to receive a 40 per cent return on this investment from the Government in the form of grant in aid and being allowed to charge a portion against excess profits.

14 UCS1/9/193. Various papers including a Memorandum and Minute from the Controller to Messrs John Brown & Co Ltd, dated 20 April 1918.

15 Ibid.

16 UCS 1/24/34. Letter from Admiralty dated 18 October 1918.

17 *Glasgow Herald* Trade Review, Saturday 28 December 1918, page 29.

18 See Table 2.

19 UCS1/9/193. Various papers including a prepared statement on the work of John Brown & Co carried out during the First World War.

20 In addition to new construction, the Company pointed out that they also built 50 hulls for Mk IV tanks, had to manage the design change from direct drive to geared turbines and carried out repair work on *Crescent, Pelorus, Mameluke, Tarpon, Scout* and three K class submarines. See UCS1/9/193.

PRE-WAR

Vessels begun before but completed during WWI

KEEL LAYINGS	
Aquitania	5 June 1911
Tiger	20 June 1912
Barham	24 February 1913
LAUNCHES	
Aquitania	21 April 1913
Tiger	15 December 1913

Left: The absence of deck beams in this magnificent view
of *Aquitania*'s hull structure gives some idea of the size of
this ship and the massive strength of the frames reducing in
size as they rise. Although the beams are yet to be fitted the
'knees' or brackets are in place ready to receive them.
A considerable amount of pre-assembly work has been
undertaken in the shops, as various parts of the structure
lying on the double bottom, not yet erected, have already
been built up into larger components. (UCS1-118-409-74)

Left: One of the very first photographs taken at Clydebank shipyard, this shows rivet squads at work in the hull of the Inman liner *City of New York* on 19 July 1887. (Author's collection)

Above: Progress of Construction photography included capturing vessel during trials at sea. This is the *Devonshire* class cruiser *Antrim* in May 1905. (Author's collection)

Above: The *Acorn* class destroyer *Brisk* running trials on the Clyde in May 1911. *Brisk* was the first destroyer to be powered by Brown–Curtis turbines in a two-shaft arrangement rather than the Parsons' type on three shafts. (UCS1-118-395-3)

Left: John Brown & Co constructed a Ship Experiment Tank at Clydebank in 1903, where scale models of ship hulls were tested to enhance hull performance. Here an upturned wax model, cast in a clay mould, is at an early stage of being brought to the exact contours of the proposed hull. Once shaped, the wax hull was towed in the tank, in order to measure its hydrodynamic efficiency. The tank was 400 feet long with an additional 45 feet to dock the models. (UCS1-118-409-3)

Below: A Japanese naval delegation, including Admiral Togo, visited Clydebank on 12 July 1911 as part of a wider tour of the area which included a visit to Barr & Stroud, makers of the rangefinders that had been fitted on Japanese warships at the Battle of Tsushima in 1905. There was a lot to interest the Japanese in British technology, including at Clydebank the Brown–Curtis turbine. The party has been photographed in front of *Aquitania*'s keel, although a visit to the battlecruiser *Australia*, then on the stocks, would have been included. (UCS1-118-409-26)

Right: *Aquitania* was the largest ship then to have been constructed at Clydebank. Her size required the building berth to be enlarged, including the driving of additional piles to support the hull, especially at the stern, as seen in this view dated 6 June 1911. The keel blocks are in position and the first plates of the ship's keel have been laid. Note the steel derrick crane lying on its side at left waiting to be erected and the rail mounted steam crane lifting keel plates into place. The ship on the stocks at right is probably the Federal Steam Navigation's *Wiltshire*, launched on 19 December 1911. (UCS1-118-409-18)

Above: Taken from the steam crane on 11 August 1911, this photograph shows the forward section of *Aquitania*'s vertical keel being erected. Sections of the vertical keel will have been riveted in the shops. The horizontal outer bottom plates have been temporarily bolted in place while an Arrol patented hydraulic riveter, supported by the steam crane, is closing a line of rivets. Activity at the building berth is constantly evolving as the ship begins to grow. Note the temporary nature of the railway track the steam crane is running along. (UCS1-118-409-38)

Below: John Brown had built many destroyers before the First World War began. Here *Acasta* takes to the water on 10 September 1912 with the paddle tug *Flying Wizard* in attendance. The new covered building berth can be seen in the background, although *Acasta* was launched from one of the berths to the right equipped with simple pole derricks. Sister ship *Achates* can be seen on the building slip. William Beardmore's shipyard at Dalmuir can be made out in the distance. (UCS1-118-412-1)

Above: John Brown's photographer was not averse to photographing ships from other shipbuilders, as in this image of the Fairfield-built battlecruiser *New Zealand* passing Clydebank on 16 September 1912. When this photograph was taken, *New Zealand*'s sister ship *Australia* was behind the photographer in the fitting-out basin, having been delayed for five months due to labour shortages and a lockout of boilermakers. (UCS1-118-OLD RED-251-1)

Above: The handsome *Empress of Russia*, built for Canadian Pacific Steamships by Fairfield's, seen here passing Clydebank in March 1913 and soon to sail on her maiden voyage from Liverpool to Vancouver via Suez and Hong Kong. (UCS1-118-OLD RED-256-14)

A spectacular wide-angle view of *Aquitania* on 20 April 1913 seen from Newshot Island, one day before her launch. The staging has gone from her hull and the drag chains have been attached. The battlecruiser *Australia* is in the fitting-out basin nearing completion. A paddle tug and a hopper, which has been used to remove material dredged from the launching run, stand by. (UCS1-118-409-319)

Below: Great care and attention was paid to launching arrangements, as seen in the massive timber structure of the after starboard poppet, or cradle, which will take the weight of *Aquitania*, in this photograph taken on 20 April 1913. The poppet is located immediately underneath a length of heavy angle iron riveted to the ship's side solely for this purpose and which will be removed after the launch. The timber props supporting the hull are being removed. Unlike warships, the shafting on many merchant vessels was enclosed in a structure faired into the hull. (UCS1-118-409-220)

Right: Position is everything. A group of unidentified men, possibly Cunard managers together with bowler-hatted shipyard counterparts, pose in front of *Aquitania*, almost, but not quite, the largest ship in the world. Behind them the launching platform is being prepared for the big event. (UCS1-118-409-184)

Left: Freshly painted, *Aquitania*'s counter stern on the day of her launch, 21 April 1913. Counter sterns were soon to become unfashionable giving way to the cruiser stern. (UCS1-118-409-212)

Right: At 12.30pm on 21 April 1913 *Aquitania* was launched by the Countess of Derby, with a reported 100,000 people watching, some of whom can be seen by the building berth. Billed as the largest ship in the world, the three *Imperator* class liners built for Hamburg America were actually a little larger. With the first anniversary of the *Titanic* disaster just eight days earlier, Cunard were anxious to stress that *Aquitania* was fully compliant with new regulations brought into force in light of the disaster, including lifeboat accommodation for all and watertight bulkheads that rose 19 feet above the waterline. (UCS1-118-409-209)

Left: No 1 berth at the east end of the shipyard on 3 October 1913 showing work on *Barham*. Several bulkheads are in place including No 68, which is nearest the camera. B gun mounting will be immediately in front of this bulkhead and the first of the boiler rooms behind. (UCS1-118-424-13)

Below: A low-pressure turbine rotor for *Aquitania* being lifted by the 150-ton derrick crane on the east quay from the bogies which had transported it from the erecting shop, 14 November 1913. The rotor weighed about 125 tons. At right, the wheel for the engine turning gear is visible, whilst at the left the coupling to the thrust shaft (at the forward end of the engine) can be seen. The slings by which the rotor is being lifted are kept vertical by means of the spreader beam directly connected to the hoist block of the crane by the upper set of slings. The rotors and casings of direct drive, low-pressure turbine machinery such as this were very much larger than those employed in the geared turbine installations that were to follow just a few years later. (UCS1-118-409-283)

Right: Perhaps an image more readily associated with shipbreaking than shipbuilding, this view looking forward taken on 19 November 1913 shows the space left open over *Aquitania*'s engine room to allow turbines and condensers to be lowered into position. Part of a turbine can be seen at lower right. The ship's four boiler rooms, one under each funnel, are forward of the engine room and are in place, and the decks above them closed up and funnels installed. When fitted, the decks above the engine room will accommodate Second Class accommodation and the Second Class Dining Saloon. Above that, approximately on a level with the camera, will be First Class staterooms and, on the uppermost deck, the First Class Smoking Room. (UCS1-118-409-266)

Below: *Aquitania*'s port low-pressure direct drive turbine partly assembled in the erecting shop with the rotor clearly visible, taken on 12 November 1913. The drum-like casting at the right end of the forged steel rotor shaft is one of the changeover valves while below that the multi-collared thrust shaft is visible. At left, a temporary adaptor is bolted to the main coupling which will connect the turbine to the propeller via intermediate and tail shafts. Turbine casings waiting to be machined are lying in the foreground (UCS1-118-409-238)

1914

KEEL LAYINGS

Milne	17 January
Moorsom	27 February
Morris	26 March
Medea	6 April
Medusa	6 April
Platypus	6 April
Pegasus	21 May
Mons	30 September
Marne	30 September
Canterbury	14 October
E35	7 December
Rigorous	22 September
Mameluke	23 December
Ossory	23 December

LAUNCHES

Milne	5 October
Morris	19 November
Moorsom	20 December
Barham	31 December
Canterbury	21 December

COMPLETIONS

Aquitania	18 May
Tiger	3 October
Milne	7 December
Morris	31 December

Left: Looking forward along the starboard side of *Barham* at main deck level from the vicinity of frame 228 on 27 March. Deck plates, including the angled ones, have been bolted into position, or 'screwed up' as it was termed, prior to riveting. Issues of fit affected shipbuilding as much as they do today. Note the turnbuckle at right of centre being used to draw two plates together prior to riveting. The instruction painted on the plate nearest to the camera says 'ringed holes to be one and an eighth + gullied over'. (UCS1-118-424-38)

Above: Once the largest and fastest
Atlantic liner, the former Cunard
Campania is seen here passing
Clydebank in 1914, almost at the end
of her life and sailing in the colours of
the Anchor Line. The ship was sold for
scrap later that year but reprieved by
the Admiralty and converted into a
seaplane carrier by Cammell Laird,
entering service in 1916. She was sunk
in an accident on the Firth of Forth
after being struck by the battleship
Royal Oak on 5 November 1918.
(UCS1-118-OLD RED-249-6)

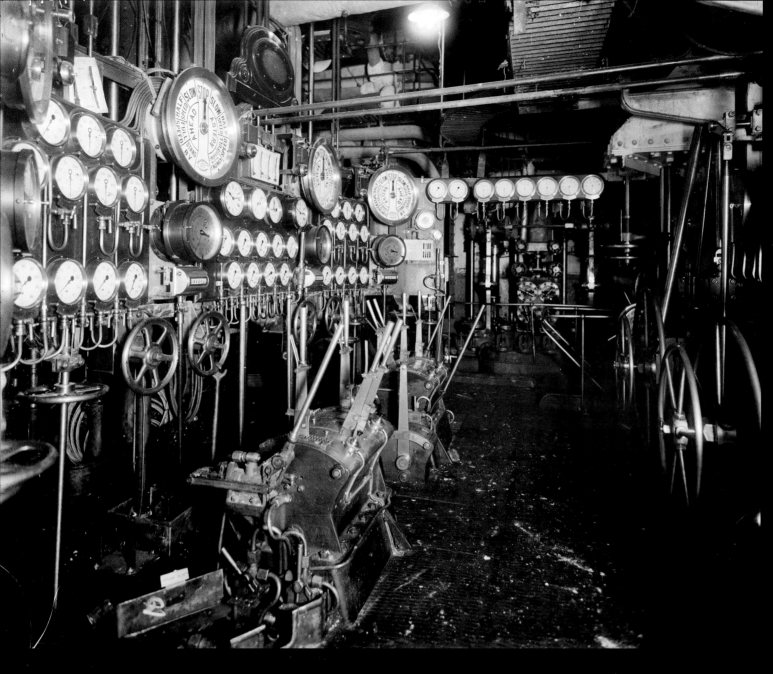

Above: *Aquitania*'s main engine control platform, photographed on 2 April, where typically the chief engineer would supervise his engineering staff in propelling the ship. The main steam valves, two concentric large diameter wheels which control the flow of steam to the turbines, are to the right. On the left, there are a myriad of gauges and controls, the most obvious of which are four Chadburn's engine telegraphs. Directly below these are the tachometers which indicate the speed at which each shaft is revolving and directly below the tachometers are the revolution counters which indicate the number of revolutions made, typically, during a four-hour watch. On the left-hand panel at centre top, an ornate wooden base awaits the maker's plate. Work in this area has not been completed, as seen by its unkempt nature. It is fair to assume that it would be gleaming by the time the ship was handed over to Cunard. (UCS1-118-409-377)

An undated image, probably taken sometime in March 1914, showing the battlecruiser *Tiger* and *Aquitania* in the fitting-out basin. Work has begun painting *Aquitania*'s superstructure in preparation for a May departure, while a large number of fitting-out trades and subcontractors will be busily completing interiors. *Tiger*, with her foremast tripod fitted, is in the early stages of fitting-out, having been launched on 15 December. This view also shows the very different 150-ton fitting-out cranes employed at Clydebank. At right is a derrick-type crane built by Cowans Sheldon of Carlisle in 1904 and, at left, a giant cantilever crane built in 1907 by Sir William Arrol & Co of Glasgow. The later remains at this site to this day. (UCS1-118-409-322)

Left: *Aquitania* and 34 of her semi-collapsible lifeboats on the dockside waiting their turn to be lifted onboard on 2 April. These boats were made by Hugh McLean of Glasgow. The ship is in the final stages of completion with painting underway and lifeboats being rigged. At the end of March, Thomas Bell, Clydebank's Managing Director, commented that while he was confident that his portion of the work would be completed by the middle of May, the various Cunard subcontractors for decorations, electric lighting and ventilation were 'having a terrific scramble'. (UCS1-118-409-368)

Above: Looking forward along *Aquitania*'s starboard side on 10 May. Only a few minor items remain to be completed as the ship is readied for departure. (UCS1-118-409-364)

Below: *Aquitania* moving slowly down the Clyde on a foggy Sunday, guided by four tugs forward and two aft. Although not visible, tens of thousands of people have lined the river to watch her go down to the sea. She anchored in the Mersey on 14 May, was dry-docked the following day, and handed over to Cunard on the 18th. Her maiden voyage from Liverpool to New York was on 30 May. After just three round trips, she was requisitioned by the Admiralty for service as an armed merchant cruiser, later being used as a troop transport and a hospital ship. (UCS1-118-GEN-290-5)

Left: Another view taken on 10 May. Note the man sitting on the ventilator cowl, which has still to be erected. (UCS1-118-409-364)

Left: Progress on *Barham* just over two weeks later on 14 April, looking towards the stern from much the same position as the previous image. Right aft, the height of the newly erected stern casting indicates the level of the quarterdeck. (UCS1-118-424-40)

Above: *Barham*: looking forward from frame 220. A rivet squad of three men working an Arrol hydraulic riveting machine pose for the camera. Supported by a crane, these machines were useful where good access to both sides of steelwork could be made. Otherwise, hand riveting applied until later in the First World War when pneumatic rivet guns were introduced. Riveters were employed on 'piecework' rates where they were paid by the amount of rivets driven. To ensure that each squad was paid correctly, a man known as a 'counter', usually a man from the time office, painted a circle around each rivet to show that it had been counted. Although captured in black and white, the reality of this image would have been highly colourful as different colours were used to mark different days of work. (Author's collection)

Above: John Brown's shipyard decked in bunting and flags in readiness for the visit by King George V on 8 July 1914. A Clyde paddle steamer is heading down river past the battleship *Barham* on the stocks at right and the battlecruiser *Tiger* in the fitting-out basin. (UCS1-118-GEN-290-7)

Right: The moment when King George V and his entourage, on board the Clyde paddle steamer *Duchess of Rothesay*, enter John Brown's fitting-out basin on 8 July. The yard has been decorated with flags flying from cranes and ships alike. The 150-ton giant cantilever crane is holding a 13.5-inch gun barrel in approximate position over B turret for dramatic effect, while *Tiger*'s forecastle is thick with men. Judging by the number of 'bunnets' being raised, three cheers for the King has just been called. (UCS1-118-276-12)

Right: The five-masted steel-hulled barque *France*, fully laden, passing John Brown's shipyard on 3 August 1914, the day before war was declared. Completed a year earlier by Chantiers et Ateliers de la Gironde at Bordeaux, *France* was at that time the second largest sailing ship ever built. This image shows the somewhat incongruous rural setting of the shipyard overseen by cattle and all manner of wildlife. The south bank of the Clyde, unlike the north at this point, was never industrialised. *France* is assisted by the screw tug *Flying Swallow* and the paddle tug *Flying Scotsman*. (UCS1-118-GEN-372-7)

Above: The West Yard on 4 August 1914, the day Britain declared war on Germany, and the destroyers that would dominate production at Clydebank much in evidence. Five destroyers are under construction, two in the covered berths, of which one is *Milne*. The others are *Medea, Medusa, Moorsom* and *Morris* – it is not clear which is which. Heavy side and barbette armour plates, probably for *Barham*, have been stored near the bow of the destroyer at right. At the base of the covered berth by the river, a solitary soldier is already on guard duty, standing on a wooden platform rigged for this purpose. Although the covered berths were new, the rest of the West Yard was old by the standards of the day, using simple steel pole derricks on the building slips with a maximum lift of 3 tons. (UCS1-118-GEN-372-1)

Left: The after section of *Tiger* photographed on 2 October 1914. Two men working off a pontoon are touching up paintwork, and what looks like ammunition boxes are stacked between Y turret and her aftermost 6-inch gun. (UCS1-118-418-149)

Below: *Tiger* with boilers fired and venting steam on 2 October. She left Clydebank on 4 October at 11am. (UCS1-118-418-138)

Above: Launch of the destroyer *Milne,* 5 October 1914. The ship is well on her way to completion, with boilers and machinery already on board. The paddle tug *Flying Elf* is standing by while further downriver two men in a rowing boat with a flag are there to stop river traffic until the launch is over. The reason for the substantial wooden fence around the West Yard berths is unclear, as security seems unlikely given the open nature of the yard. The control top of the battleship *Benbow* can be made out underneath the crane in Beardmore's Naval Construction Works in the middle distance. (UCS1-118-426-1)

Right: Midships view of *Milne* taken on 15 December 1914 and most likely at the same time as the above. Note that the destroyer has been painted black overall. (UCS1-118-426-8)

Below: The M class destroyer *Milne* in December 1914 during her trials
programme. This began on 25 November and was completed on 7 December when
she left Clydebank for the last time, making her the first destroyer to be completed
during wartime. The rails fitted on the starboard side leading to the stern are
something of a mystery, but can only be associated with minelaying. At this early
stage in the war, minelaying was in its infancy and it could be that the arrangement
at *Milne*'s stern was experimental. The Russian cruiser *Askold* is lying at the other
side of the basin, possibly in connection with Brown–Curtis machinery parts
manufactured at Clydebank for the two Russian battleships *Imperatritsa Mariya* and
Imperator Aleksandr III, under construction in the Black Sea. (UCS1-118-426-6)

Above: On the last day of 1914, *Barham* is launched, the fourth of the *Queen Elizabeth* class to do so. The shipyard diary for this date states:

'No 424 Barham launched at 12 noon. In addition to the luncheon for guests, a luncheon was provided in the Moulding Loft for foremen and several members of the staff, Mr Luke presiding. The Works close today for New Year holidays. To enable employees to view the launch, work will cease on sounding the whistle at 11.30am. (time workers being paid up to 12 noon as usual) Wages, reckoned up to Tuesday 29th at 5.30pm, will be paid on sounding of the whistle for a second time at noon shortly after the launch. Night shift will stop at 5.30am when wages will be paid.'

(UCS1-118-424-140)

Right: John Brown's Army. Soon after the outbreak of war John Brown & Co established a company of soldiers known locally as the Dunbartonshire Volunteers, but who were an informal Volunteer Training Corps unit. Their drums are marked Argyll and Sutherland Highlanders, suggesting a relationship with this local infantry regiment. In this view taken in late 1914, officers, NCOs and men, including pipers and drummers, have formed up outside one of the plater's sheds. A set of plate rolls with associated crane to lift plates is visible in the background. In July 1916, the company was recognised by the Army and then able to take over the duties of the Military Guard, hitherto responsible for protecting the shipyard. The cost of clothing and equipping the company of 130 men was £1000, to be charged against excess profits. The Volunteers were disbanded in February 1918. (UCS1-118-GEN-289-5)

1915

KEEL LAYINGS

E36	7 January
Repulse	25 January
Platypus	6 April
Penn	9 June
Peregrine	9 June
E50	26 June
Napier	6 July
Narbrough	13 July
Romola	25 August
Rowena	25 August
Restless	22 September
Rigorous	22 September

LAUNCHES

Medea	30 January
Medusa	27 March
Mons	1 May
Marne	29 May
Mameluke	14 August
Ossory	9 October
Napier	27 November
Canterbury	21 December

COMPLETIONS

Moorsom	17 February
Medea	22 June
Medusa	1 July
Mons	14 July
Marne	14 July
Barham	26 August
Mameluke	31 October
Ossory	4 December

Left: The *Lord Clive* class monitor *Prince Rupert*, seen here on 24 May, was built at Port Glasgow by Wm Hamilton & Co Ltd. She was brought upriver to Clydebank on 20 May 1915 to have her twin 12-inch gun mounting fitted by the 150-ton derrick crane. In this view taken over *Barham*'s secondary guns, her barbette is complete and her 12-inch turret and guns are visible on the quayside above and slightly forward of her quarterdeck. (UCS1-118-GEN-335-7)

Below: The starboard low-pressure Brown-Curtis turbine for *Barham* in the erecting shop on 6 January 1915. On the left is the LP (low-pressure) ahead turbine and on the right is the LP astern turbine rotor minus its casing. The port and starboard LP sets occupied the centre engine room with high-pressure (HP) ahead and astern turbines in independent wing engine rooms. The steam inlet from the HP turbine can be seen in the large flanges (with protective timber covers by the full figure engineer), while the flat top to the ahead turbine at left indicates the exhaust to condenser. Main bearing top covers are visible in the foreground. (UCS1-118-424-281)

Right: Seen on 8 February, five weeks after her launch, work fitting out *Barham* is well under way. The foremast has been fitted, A barbette armour has been erected, and the armoured vertical communication tube in the conning tower can be seen. The base of the fore funnel has been built with square, armoured gratings visible in the after funnel space. Teak deck planks are stacked on the forecastle ready to be laid, while numerous fittings such as hatches, coamings for watertight doors, etc, are scattered throughout. (UCS1-118-424-159)

Left: The M class destroyer *Moorsom* stopped on the Firth of Clyde during trials in February 1915. Her trials programme began on 1 February and involved five subsequent departures from the shipyard to the Firth of Clyde and back again and one trip to the dry-dock at Govan before her last trial began on 17 February. This undated photograph was most likely taken early in the trials programme, as the black paint scheme to be applied to her hull is incomplete. (Author's collection)

Below: *Barham*'s Y turret turntable being lifted from the quayside into position on the ship on 9 March. Note the embrasure for the aftermost port 6-inch gun which is yet to be plated over as these mountings were later suppressed. The 150-ton derrick crane is in the background. (UCS1-118-424-183)

Right: This striking waterline view
demonstrates the photographer's desire
to achieve something more than a
record shot. The image, taken on
18 March shows a net defence boom
placed over the mouth of the fitting-
out basin. *Barham* is on the far quay
wall while the stern of the Clyde
Navigation Trust's Hopper No 4, used
to remove excavate, is on the near wall.
Dredging the fitting-out basin was
required on a routine basis. In the
background, the covered shipbuilding
gantry is being doubled in size in
response to the growing number of
destroyer contracts. (UCS1-118-424-178)

Left: *Barham*'s 15-inch gun mountings were manufactured by Vickers at Barrow and brought to Clydebank on the coaster *Aydon* between 24 February and 12 March. In this view taken on 12 April both X and Y are in the later stages of construction with the trunk, turntable and other parts of the mountings already installed and the turrets being built up. (UCS1-118-424-208)

Below: By 20 April when this photograph was taken, Y gun house is all but complete, with the exception of the roof plates. The guns are still supported on wooden blocks at the muzzles. X gun house has been built up and awaits its guns. (UCS1-118-424-215)

Above: On 6 April 1914 two destroyers, *Kriti* and *Lesvos*, of a broadly similar design to contemporary British M class destroyers, were laid down at Clydebank for the Greek Government. The TBDs were part of a four-ship order taken over by the Admiralty in September, the other two of which were under construction at Fairfield. *Kriti* was launched on 30 January 1915 and *Lesvos* on 27 March 1915. This was a long time for ships of this type to be on the stocks and probably reflects changes to the design to bring them into line with British practice. In May 1915 the ships were given the names *Medea* (ex *Kriti*) and *Medusa*. They are seen here in the fitting-out basin on 21 April 1915 minus armament, still bearing their Greek names at the stern. Note the rails at the stern on the starboard side, possibly an early means of minelaying. The name boards on the building at the head of the basin carrying the shipbuilder's name have been painted out, perhaps as a security measure. (UCS1-118-GEN-342-7)

Right: The keel and after section of *Repulse* on 21 April. The cast steel stern frame will be attached to the keel at this point. To the left, the large diameter holes are where the port inner and outer shafts will run. In the foreground, preassembled sections await erection. (Author's collection)

Right: In this view of *Repulse* taken on 26 April the photographer has positioned himself close to frame 284 looking forward. The men nearest the camera are on the inner bottom plating, the structure of which has been bolted together prior to riveting. The steel work with large diameter holes to either side will form the tunnels for the innermost propeller shafts. In the distance, bulkhead 197 has been erected which will separate the engine room from the boiler room, the latter of which will be on the far side. The bulkhead is marked 'Dalzell Steel' indicating that it was made at the Motherwell works of David Colville & Co. The heavy framework on either side of this bulkhead and running towards the stern is for the anti-torpedo bulges. The 15-inch magazine for Y turret will be located on the deck, immediately above the position occupied by the camera and where the men have stopped for the camera. (UCS1-118-443-10)

Left: Planking *Barham*'s boat deck is almost complete in this photograph taken on 4 May 1915. Note the searchlight platform at the base of the after funnel and the two engine room vents immediately abaft the funnel. The light wooden framing on the port side supported a canvas cover to permit all-weather working. Note the triangular structure, part of the shelter deck, at the base of the main mast, which housed officers' ward rooms. (UCS1-118-424-228)

Right: *Barham*'s secondary armament has been fitted, while work on the forward turrets is about to start. (UCS1-118-424-224)

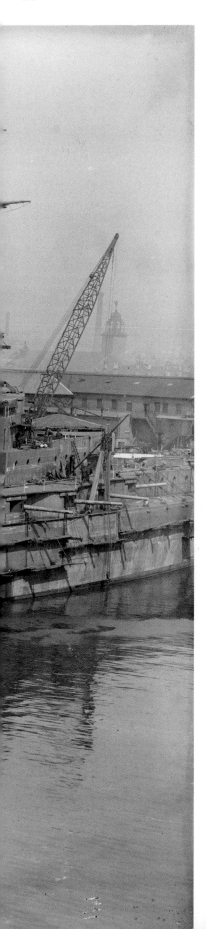

Left: This view, also taken on 4 May, shows the aftermost 6-inch embrasures on the main deck ready to receive mountings which, in the event, were never fitted, because they were considered to be too close to the water to be of much value in action. Abreast the main mast, a heavy timber A frame has been stepped on the deck above the area where a 13-inch plate from the ship's side armour has either been removed or not yet fitted. Y turret bears quite a few hand-painted inscriptions which reflect issues of the day: 'How is the Kaiser like Holland? Because he is a lowlife and is well damned'. Another proclaims 'Home Rule for Yoker' – a nearby district of Glasgow. (UCS1-118-424-227)

Below: The last major element in the construction of *Barham* was the installation of the main armament. This added many thousands of tons to the weight of the ship, which was otherwise structurally complete with machinery and boilers already installed. Final alignment of the shafting would be completed after the aftermost mountings were fitted, in case the great weight caused hull deflection. For this reason the aftermost mountings were generally fitted first. In this 7 May view, Y turret has been completed while the last 15-inch gun for X turret is being slowly lowered onto its cradle at a maximum speed of 5 feet per minute. The roof plate is lying on the quayside beside the Scotch boilers. In the background, four destroyers, one cruiser and one submarine are under construction. (UCS1-118-424-231)

Above: *Prince Rupert*'s port quarter on 24 May, seen over the stern of *Medea*, which still bears her Greek name at the stern. *Prince Rupert*'s 12-inch mounting was surrendered from the *Majestic* class battleship *Victorious* and modified at Elswick to increase elevation from 13.5 degrees to 30 degrees. *Barham* is on the West Quay. (UCS1-118-GEN-335-6)

Below: Later that day, in this view, *Prince Rupert*'s turret and guns have been installed. (UCS1-118-GEN-335-5)

Left: This photograph of *Barham*, taken on 7 June from the conning tower, affords a good view inside both A and B barbettes, of which A is more advanced, with the mounting installed and the floor of the gun house fitted on top of the working chamber. However, B barbette shows more of the barbette structure with, at the bottom, the ring bulkhead (honeycombed structure), and above that in sequence, the training rack and the roller path that will take the 760-ton weight of revolving mounting including guns. Note the 10-inch thick barbette armour. From the breakwater forward, the forecastle appears to be complete with capstan gear, hatches and anchor chains in place. (UCS1-118-424-234)

Right, upper: A 100-ton 15-inch gun being lifted onto its cradle in *Barham*'s A turret on 18 June. The second barrel is lying on the quayside partially obscured by wooden crates. Turret roof plates are also stored there. A gun cradle is lying to the extreme right of shot. This was the day on which Lord Fisher, recently resigned as First Sea Lord over disagreements with Churchill about the Gallipoli campaign, visited Clydebank to see progress on the battlecruiser *Repulse*, a ship he had done much to bring into being. (UCS1-118-424-240)

Right, lower: 18 June. *Medea*, nearest the camera, is almost complete with three 4-inch QF guns and two twin 21-inch torpedo tubes installed. With just four days to go until her departure from Clydebank, *Medea* is wearing her final top coat of paint. Black had been customary for destroyers although this changed to grey during 1915. *Medusa* is lying inboard of *Medea* and still without her armament. Although launched nearly two months after her sister, *Medusa* was completed and left Clydebank just eight days after *Medea* on 1 July 1915. (Author's collection)

Right: Charles Duncan, Labour MP for Barrow in Furness, is about to address workers at John Brown's on 3 August, almost one year after the outbreak of war. Duncan, an engineer by trade, served an apprenticeship at Armstrong's Elswick Ordnance Works, and was General Secretary of the Workers Union. (UCS1-118-GEN-397-1)

Above: In what looks like a race down the Clyde to the open sea, the monitor *M4* (soon to be renamed *Raglan*) is being overtaken by the Yarrow-built M class destroyer *Moon*. This scene was captured by John Brown's photographer on 21 June as the vessels were passing Clydebank. *M4* made use of US-built 14-inch turrets and guns, which were intended for the Greek battlecruiser *Salamis* under construction by AG Vulkan in Hamburg. After the outbreak of war the maker of the mountings, Bethlehem Steel, not wishing to break the British blockade of Germany, sold all four to the British instead, who designed the four ships of the *Abercrombie* class around them. (Author's collection)

Right: Crew members gathering on *Barham*'s forecastle deck by X turret on 19 August. Blast bags are being fitted to the guns in Y turret with X turret's bags almost in place. Note the 6-inch gun embrasures abreast and below the after turrets have now been plated over. (UCS1-118-424-245)

FROM THIS PLATFORM
AT 9.20. A.M. ON TUESDAY 31ST AUGUST
MR CHARLES DUNCAN
(LABOUR M.P. FOR BARROW)
SUPPORTED BY { MR A.A. ALLEN, M.P.
& MR D.H.L. YOUNG }
WILL SPEAK ON THE TOPIC OF "THE DAY"

Above and following pages: Four views of *Barham* taken on 26 August.
The quarterdeck on the day she left the shipyard to run trials. The White Ensign is
flying from the ensign gaff stepped immediately abaft the armoured torpedo
director tower. (UCS1-118-424-253)

Above: The boat deck seen from the 150-ton cantilever crane. (UCS1-118-424-249)

Above: Midships looking forward from
crane. The destroyer *Mameluke* is on the
east side of the basin.
(UCS1-118-424-248)

Below: With just two days to go before departure, the ship's crew is putting her in order. Rigging the stays on the forward funnel is still underway, while on the starboard side, a cutter is about to be lifted onto its cradles. Canvas screens around various platforms are in place as well as splinter mats on the compass platform. (UCS1-118-424-255)

Left: *Repulse* was brought to the
launching stage in a remarkably short
time. In this view, taken on
29 December 1915, the forward poppet
on the starboard side is being built up
as a works saddle tank locomotive
passes by. (UCS1-118-443-153)

Above: Although most of the machinery for the battlecruiser *Furious* (under
construction at Armstrong Whitworth's on the Tyne) was being manufactured by the
Wallsend Slipway, this turbine was switched to John Brown at Clydebank, most likely
because of capacity issues and the urgency with which *Furious* was required. The first
thing to notice about this turbine, which is of the Brown-Curtis type, is its small size
in comparison to the turbine for *Barham* shown earlier. Until this time, turbines had
been direct drive, coupled directly to the propeller shaft. The introduction of geared
turbines, from which *Furious* was one of the first to benefit, allowed the turbine to
run at a much higher speed and, through a gearbox, the prop shaft was allowed to
rotate at a more efficient speed. Geared turbines used high temperature steam at a
higher pressure than direct drive turbines and this allowed the turbine to be much
smaller for a similar power output. The photograph, taken sometime in December,
shows an HP turbine, with the top casing removed, sitting on its bearings while the
wheels are in the process of having shrouds fitted – two remaining to be so fitted. In
operation, steam would enter the turbine at the left, travel along the turbine turning
the wheel and exhaust through the port at right bottom, the flange of which can be
seen resting on the wooden block. (UCS1-118-446-1)

The bow of the *Cambrian* class cruiser *Canterbury* seen on 21 December 1915 shortly before her launch, which was performed by the Hon Mrs Edward Lascelles at 12.20pm. One of four launching poppets can be seen and beneath these are the neatly arranged drag chains which will arrest the movement of the ship in the water. A launching ram has been positioned against the poppet, ready to start the ship on its launching run. She has been built under the new covered building berth, clearly not quite long enough for the 446-foot long cruiser. (UCS1-118-435-2)

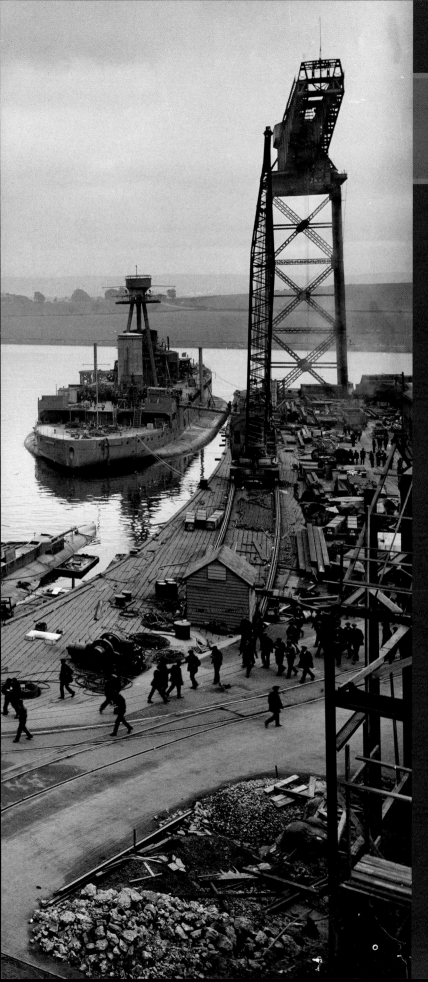

1916

KEEL LAYINGS

Skate	12 January
Tarpon	12 April
Telemachus	12 April
Ceres	26 April
Simoom	23 May
Hood	1 September
Vanoc	20 September
Vanquisher	29 September

LAUNCHES

Repulse	8 January
Narbrough	2 March
Penn	8 April
Romola	14 May
E35	20 May
Peregrine	29 May
Rowena	1 July
Restless	12 August
E36	16 September
Rigorous	30 September
Platypus	28 October
Simoom	30 October
E50	30 November

COMPLETIONS

Napier	22 January
Narborough	29 April
Canterbury	9 May
Penn	31 May
Peregrine	10 July
E35	14 July
Repulse	14 August
Romola	17 August
Rowena	29 September
Restless	21 October
E36	16 November
Rigorous	27 November
Simoom	22 December

Left: This view taken on 16 July 1916 shows *Repulse* on the East Quay with *Rowena* (forward) and *Romola*. On the West Quay, *E35* is at the head of the basin and the monitor *Erebus*, built at Harland & Wolff's Govan shipyard, is under the 150-ton giant cantilever crane waiting to have her 15-inch gun mounting shipped. *Erebus* arrived at John Brown's on 13 July, leaving five days later with the mounting installed. (Author's collection)

Left: The elegant stern of *Repulse* on 7 January 1916, one day before her launch.
The standing ways are in position with the one at left about to be covered in tallow
– a lubricant to enable the launching ways to slide over the standing ways and carry
the ship into the river. The jibs of the 5-ton derricks have been swung out of the
way in parallel with the berth. Note the props holding the standing ways in
position. (UCS1-118-443-158)

Below: The *Queen Elizabeth* class battleship *Valiant*, built by the Fairfield
Shipbuilding & Engineering Co Ltd at Govan, passing Clydebank on 5 February
1916. The crew are at the starboard side of the battleship to see ships under
construction at John Brown's. (UCS1-118-OLD RED-326-5)

Left: The *Cambrian* class cruiser *Castor* passing Clydebank on 25 February 1916. Built at Birkenhead by Cammell Laird, *Castor* was commissioned in November 1915 as flagship of the 11th Destroyer Flotilla. She is virtually identical to Clydebank's *Canterbury*. Three months after this photograph was taken, *Castor* was in action at the Battle of Jutland where twelve of her crew lost their lives as a result of enemy fire. (UCS1-118-GEN-372-2)

Right: The vessel at the centre of this picture is the turbine steamer *Queen Alexandria*, built by Wm Denny & Co at Dumbarton in 1912 to the order of Turbine Steamers Ltd, for the Greenock to Campbeltown service. Although undated, the presence of *Repulse* and *Canterbury* indicate late March 1916, by which time *Queen Alexandria* had been in service as a troop transport for over a year. Surprisingly, she is still in her company colours which appear remarkably fresh, suggesting that she has just been painted. The men at her stern support this view as they are working on her port of registry lettering 'Glasgow'. *Queen Alexandria* would later distinguish herself by depth-charging, ramming and sinking *UB78* on 9 May 1918 off Cherbourg. (UCS1-118-GEN-260-9)

Right: Built as the Royal Mail Lines *Balantia* by Harland & Wolff, Belfast, in 1909, the ship was taken over and converted into a hospital ship after the Scottish branch of the Red Cross Society raised over £20,000. The ship, given the name *St Margaret of Scotland*, was staffed by Scottish doctors and nurses and saw service at Gallipoli and the Black Sea before returning to her former role and name. She is seen here outward bound, passing Clydebank on 14 March 1916. (UCS1-118-GEN-372-5)

Above: The *Cambrian* class light cruiser *Canterbury* in May 1916. This undated photograph, taken shortly before her departure in May 1916 to join the fleet, shows the bridge and port forward 4-inch gun. Splinter mats have been fitted around the bridge, above which is the searchlight platform fitted on the pole foremast; a second searchlight platform can be seen forward of the fore funnel. Note the signal lamp and the semaphore telegraph on the bridge wing. Members of the ship's company are already assigned and, together with John Brown's men, are working to prepare the ship for departure. The large drum lying on the deck beside the sailors dressed in whites says 'Oil Mineral Sperm'. (UCS1/118/435/11)

Left: *Canterbury*'s midships area on the port side showing fore funnel and 4-inch guns. (UCS1-118-435-21)

Right: A good view of *Canterbury*'s layout seen from the 150-ton giant cantilever fitting-out crane on 3 May. The destroyer *Penn* is lying outboard of *Canterbury* with the deck above the engine room opened up. Both ships have been moved off the quayside to allow a vessel (probably *Wolhandel*) to receive a cargo of turbine machinery for Russia. *Repulse* is on the Easy Quay having been fitted with A and B 15-inch mountings from the battleship *Resolution*. (UCS1-118-435-14)

Right: Seen over the West Yard slipways, *Canterbury* is at the start of her voyage down the Clyde. She appears to be flying the White Ensign indicating that she has been commissioned into the Navy. She is also carrying a large number of shipyard workmen and other civilian personnel, suggesting some work remained to be completed post-trials. (UCS1-118-435-26)

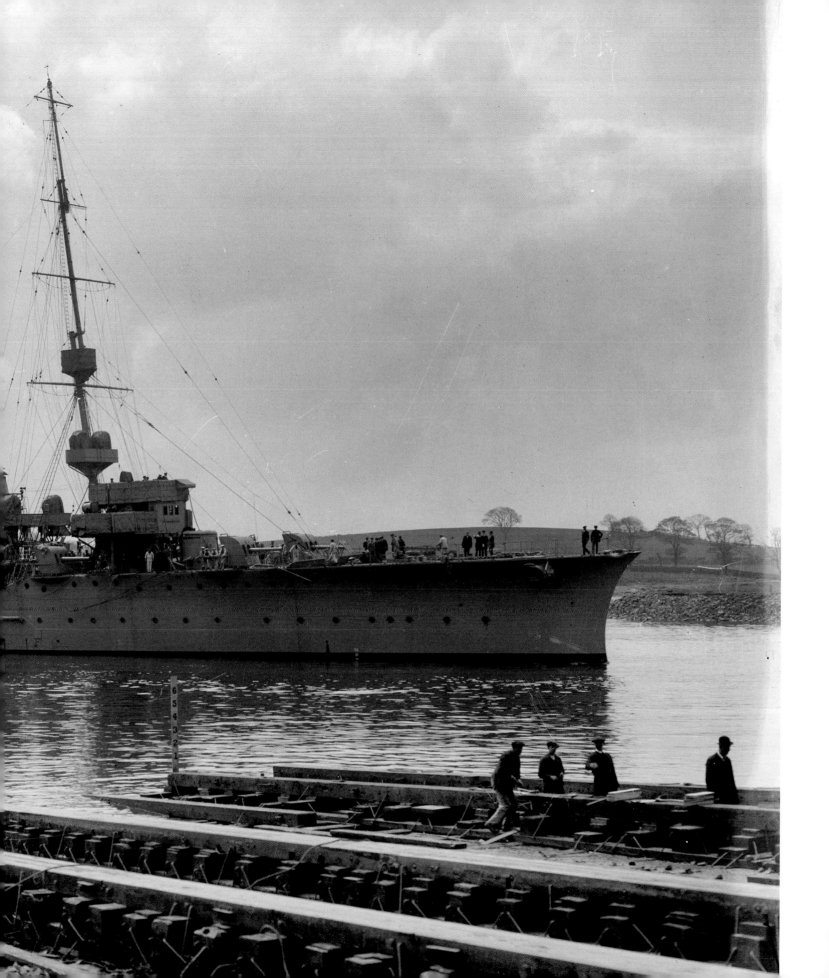

Above: In this view, taken on 22 April,
E35 is set to be the first submarine
launched at Clydebank.
Note the props and steel 'dogs' holding
the launching ways in position as well
as the launching cradle or poppet
supporting the hull. The three men
looking at the camera are shipyard
managers, as defined by their bowler
hats. (UCS1-118-436-2)

Above: Accidents do happen. Despite the successful launch of 435 vessels before it, Ship No 436, HM S/M *E35*, fell off the slipway during her launching run on 23 April 1916. According to the Shipyard Diary, the ground gave way under the standing ways causing them to collapse. Apart from a gash along the rudder, there is nothing visible to suggest serious damage although in all probability some plates and frames on the starboard external ballast tanks would have to be replaced. The submarine has been propped in this position to prevent further movement while shipyard officials decide how best to pull her upright again. (UCS1-118-436-13)

Right: *E35* launched successfully on 20 May 1916, almost one month after the launching mishap. Beardmore's shipyard is visible in the background. (UCS1-118-436-17)

Below: *E35* in the fitting-out basin on the day of her launch. With most of her equipment on board, less than two months was required to complete her. The bow of *Repulse* can be seen on the other side of the basin, at the head of which is one of her 50-foot steam pinnaces and a 42-foot motor launch. (UCS1-118-436-20)

Although warship interiors were generally never photographed, an exception was made for these undated views of *E35* but most likely taken in July 1916.

Right: *E35*'s forward torpedo room with two 18-inch torpedoes half loaded into the tubes. Overhead can be seen hoop cradles for the spare torpedoes and above them two rail girders for manhandling the torpedoes during loading. Power-assisted loading was not introduced until the end of the Second World War. The hatch on the floor to the right with the butterfly wing bolts gives access to the magazine and the curved lever on the right-hand side is for locking the folding wireless mast into position. The large rod on the right (starboard) side operates the forward hydroplanes. The trim and ballast valves are above the spare gear and tools chests at left. (UCS1-118-436-29)

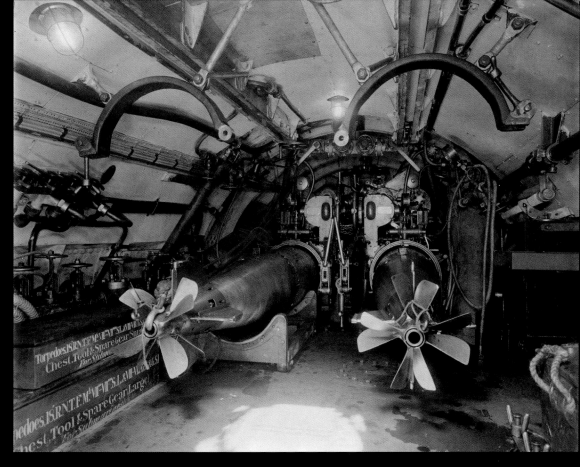

Right: The main and auxiliary electrical switchboards. The boat's main battery was immediately below this area and the air compressor further aft of this. The large pipe overhead on the right is part of the battery ventilation system. Equipment manufacturers include M.B, Whipp & Bourne, Weston Electrical Equipment Co, and Verity's Ltd. The labelled switches and fuses for all electric equipment on board are at right of shot. (UCS1-118-436-28)

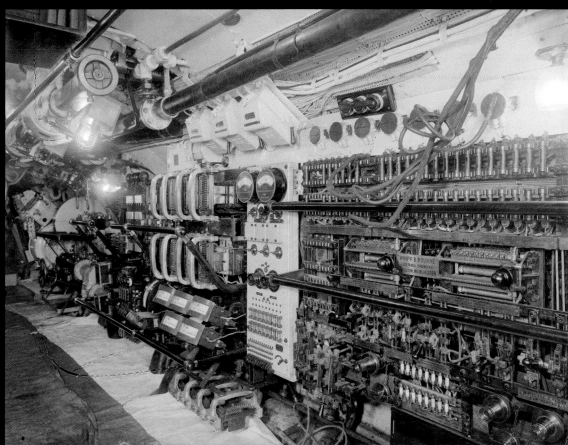

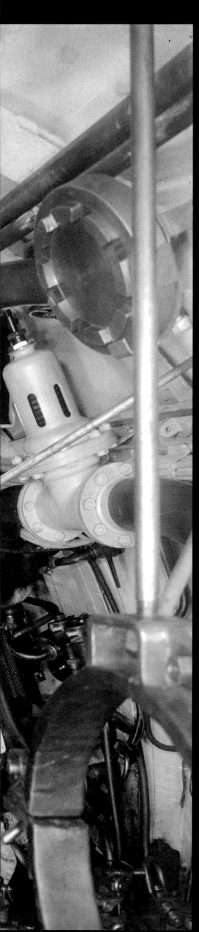

Above: Directly opposite the main switchboard are the officers' quarters, cabinets, drawers and the captain's bunk at top right, the only bunk on the boat, complete with a voice tube at the far end. A curtain rail can be seen overhead which gives some degree of privacy. To the right of this is the control rod for the forward hydroplane and, above that, pigeon holes for the boat's recognition flags. The motor overhead is for raising and lowering the periscopes. At top right behind the ornate light, a rifle hangs with bayonet fitted. These boats only had two subdivision bulkheads and the one shown forward leads into the fore ends and torpedo tubes. The large vertical pipe against the bulkhead door is the chain pipe for the forward anchor. (UCS1-118-436-30)

Left: The difficulty of fitting a lot of gear into the confined space of a submarine is clear from this shot of *E35* taken just above one of the athwartships 18-inch torpedo tubes, visible at the very bottom. The conning tower is above and slightly forward of the photographer and the main diesel engines are immediately behind. This midships position was the widest part of the boat and where, in addition to the torpedo tubes, the main controls and switchboard were located. The wheels in the centre are the rudder controls, and to the right of that behind the top-mounted gyro are the planesman's controls. Note the four voice pipes at left. The periscope is raised. Below this compartment were the submarine's main batteries and the two large vertical pipes, one on either side, are part of the battery ventilation system. The circular shape amidships at the top is a fresh air inlet pipe from the conning tower and the two circular hoops near the bottom are for stowing spare torpedoes for the beam tubes. Loading the beam torpedo tubes involved unscrewing the ringbolts seen in the photo and hinging the top half of the tube open. One of the boat's compressed air flasks used for surfacing can just be seen low down on the left side of the photo. Just forward of the conning tower ladder is the boat's gyro compass. Shipyard workers have placed the steel shaft seen in front of the ladder to support the periscope in the raised position for convenience, an arrangement that would not have been used at sea. (UCS1-118-436-25)

Below: The planesman's position looking aft with depth gauges located above the two large hydroplane wheels. Although still in the shipyard, the boat is clearly fully crewed, evidenced by the electric fan and the portable heater below. On top of the wooden desk unit there appears to be an electric kettle and, more ominously, a box with a label that says 'Government Explosives'. On the bulkhead to the right of that are two large Elliott Brothers gauges, one for Knots and the other for Distance. The area to the left of the photo is the forward end of the officers' quarters. A steel rod with curtain rings can be seen, which when fitted and drawn would offer some privacy. The shaft with universal couplings at upper left of shot operated the forward hydroplanes and above that is pigeon-hole stowage for the boat's recognition flags. There are two folding stools to the left of the heater and just behind them the bilge pump. (UCS1-118-436-7-6)

Right: With some of her crew taking it easy on the casing, *E35* slips down river on 14 July 1916 to run the first of her trials on the Gareloch. Quite a few John Brown men and other civilian contractors (men in bowler hats, soft hats and 'bunnets') are also present. A paddle tug flying John Brown's house flag is following astern. *E35* returned to the Gareloch on 17 July for further trials and left Clydebank finally on 24 July at 2pm. (Author's collection)

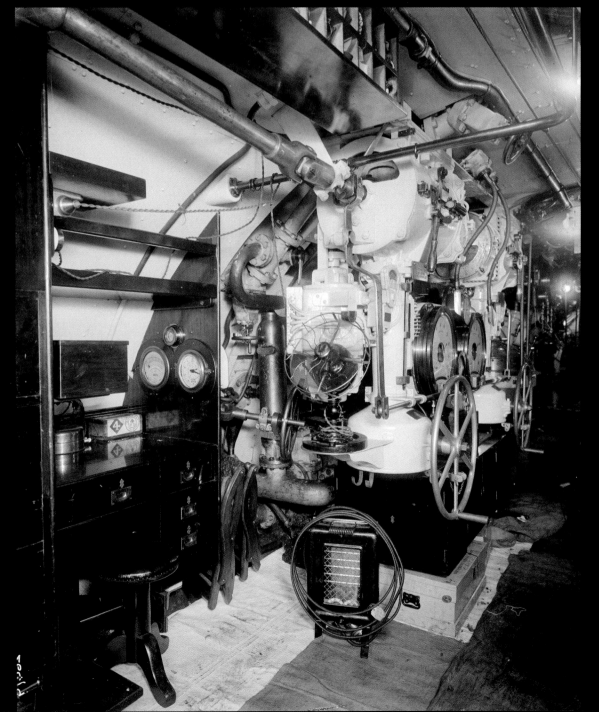

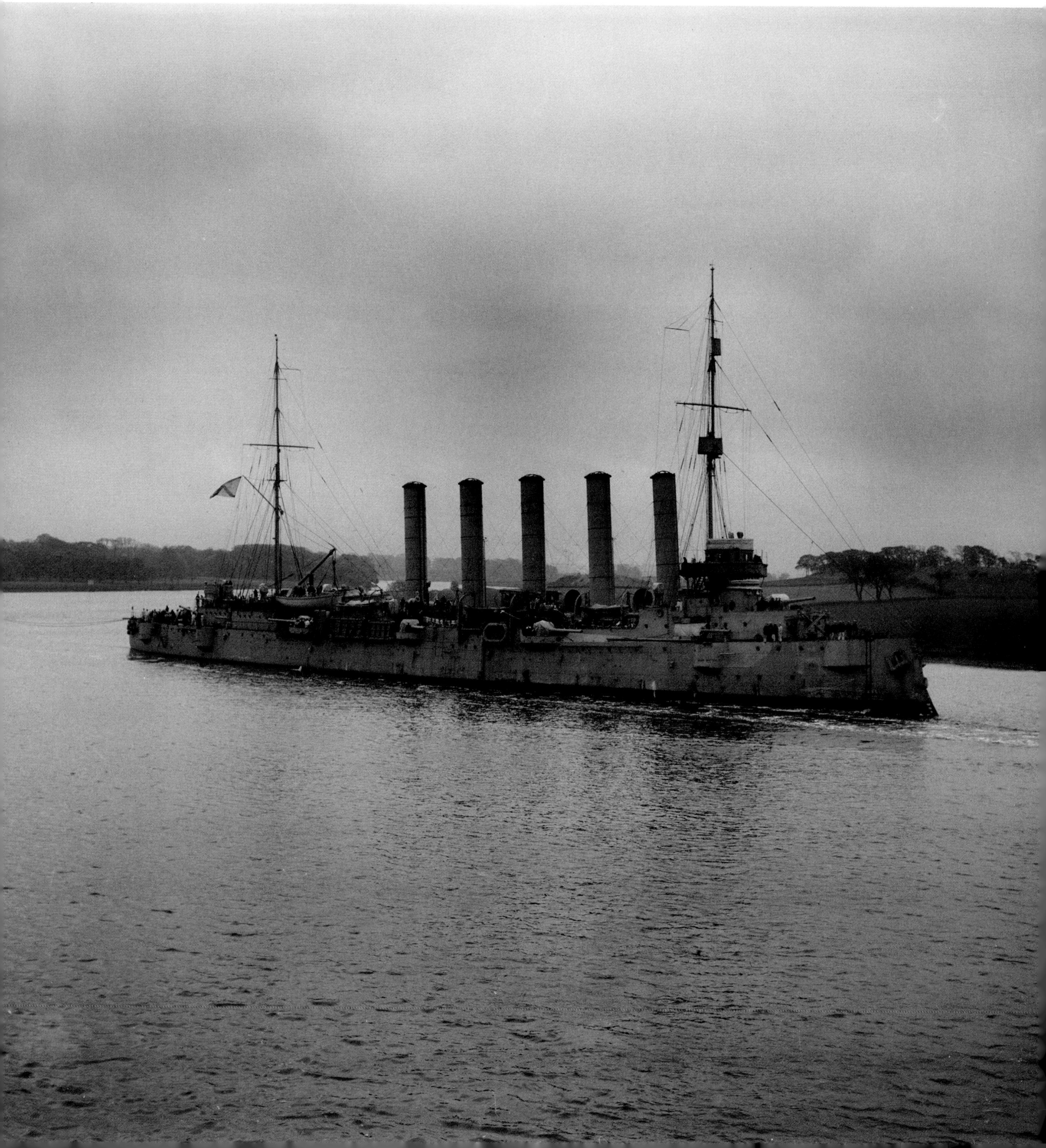

Left and above: An unlikely sight on the River Clyde brought about by war. These undated photographs are of the Russian cruiser *Askold* passing Clydebank probably taken sometime in April or May 1916. She is most likely at Clydebank in connection with the Brown-Curtis turbine machinery manufactured at Clydebank for the battleship *Imperator Aleksandr III*, under construction at Nikolaev on the Black Sea. *Askold* probably acted as escort to the merchant ship *Wolhandel* on the first leg of the journey, which was to Archangel. Thereafter, the machinery travelled down through Russia by barge, railway and steamer before reaching Nikolaev, a journey of almost 5400 miles in total since leaving Clydebank. Known by British sailors as the 'Packet of Woodbines' (cigarettes sold in fives) because of her numerous funnels, the cruiser was built in Germany in 1902, and saw service in the Russian Baltic and Pacific fleets and was present at the Battle of Tsushima. During the First World War she served in the Pacific and Mediterranean theatres, ending with service in the White Sea with the Royal Navy as *Glory IV*. (UCS1-118-GEN-260-1)

Left: A condenser being lifted into the Belgian steamer *Wolhandel* in May 1916, destined for the Black Sea and the Russian battleship *Imperator Aleksandr III*. Because of the war, the Brown–Curtis machinery installation for this battleship had to be taken to the Black Sea via Archangel and overland, rather than through the Mediterranean and the Bosporus. *Wolhandel* left Clydebank on 16 May after a journey of 5348 miles. The machinery arrived at Nikolaev on 23 October. (UCS1-118-422-3)

Above: This view of *Repulse* and the following four were taken on 12 August; it shows A and B turrets trained on the port beam. Note the splinter mats and the single 4-inch mounting abreast the conning tower. (UCS1-118-443-374)

Right: The shield for the 4-inch triple mounting fitted on the light structure abaft the main mast is being lowered into position. The 4-inch magazine and shell room to supply this mounting and the 4-inch mounting aft of it (No 5) were on the platform deck beside Y turret 15-inch magazine. The structure on the main mast bearing battle honours is the night control defence position. (UCS1-118-443-365)

Below: Looking forward along *Repulse*'s starboard side, showing details of her hull plating, night lifebuoy, booms and various other fittings. (UCS1-118-443-373)

Right: The towering structure of *Repulse*'s foremast, platforms and control top. The 32-foot cutter is being rigged with its boarding net hanging below. (UCS1-118-443-375)

Below: This photograph, also taken on 12 August, offers a detailed view of the flying deck before the 4-inch triple mounting was fitted on its ring. Going forward, there is a blast screen to protect the 4-inch gun crew and ammunition hoists. The torpedo control tower is forward of this with an incomplete 9-foot base rangefinder. Behind the blast screen can be seen the davit and sheaves situated above the ammunition trunk for hoisting 4-inch ammunition from the shell room and magazines below. The R class destroyer *Romola* lies to the left with possibly *Rowena* inboard of her, both on the west quay. *Romola* left Clydebank on 17 August, three days after *Repulse*. (UCS1-118-443-367)

Below: After a trials programme that had begun on 3 August, this view shows the R class destroyer *Romola* on 17 August going down river to begin her final trial, ending with departure to join the Fleet on that day. (Author's collection)

Left: The battlecruiser *Renown* passed Clydebank on 16 September from her builders, the Fairfield Shipbuilding & Engineering Co Ltd. The smoke along the side of the ship is from the tug out of shot to the right. *Renown* and *Repulse* were laid down on the same day in January 1915, although *Repulse* was completed one month earlier. *Renown* has just passed the confluence of the River Cart with the River Clyde. Just visible by the Cart, which can be seen in the background, is the large boiler works of Babcock & Wilcox Ltd at Renfrew. (UCS1-118-OLD RED-326-3)

Left: A detail of the forward poppet supporting the submarine tender *Platypus* on 16 October. John Brown's tender to build a submarine depot ship for the Australian Government was accepted in July 1914 and the keel laid on 6 April 1915, but the contract suspended soon after. Work resumed in May 1916 and the vessel was launched on 28 October. Note the chains around the poppet, which pass under the ship's hull to the poppet on the other side, ensuring that the poppets are kept in tight contact with the hull as the ship slides down the standing ways into the river. The men standing still while the photographer makes the exposure are probably preparing the ship for launch, which will include removal of the heavy timber shores propping the hull and securing the drag chains, already in place, to the ship's side. (UCS1-118-432-5)

Below: Dominated by the 150-ton giant cantilever crane, John Brown's third and last submarine, *E50*, is launched successfully at the first attempt on 13 November 1916. *E50* left Clydebank to complete trials on 29 January 1917. She was lost with all hands in January 1918 after striking a mine off the Danish coast. (UCS1-118-438-1)

Below: 5 September 1916. The double bottom of *Hood* on No 3 berth just five days after the keel had been laid. The reason why such rapid progress could be made was that the transverse double bottom sections had been pre-assembled in the platers' shops before the keel was laid. Some of these sections, still to be added on the berth, can be seen lying on the ground at right of shot. Many of the sections or frames in place on the berth are held together with a few bolts only, another reason for the speed of assembly. By this means, the structure of the ship can be erected quickly, lined up and propped in position before riveting begins. A rivet squad is working at left with their rivet fire standing on planks. Split tree trunks, to be used as staging once the hull sides are erected, can be seen lying on the ground on the right. (UCS1-118-460-20)

Right: The ill-fated R class destroyer *Simoom* photographed in poor light on 21 December. Launched on 30 October, *Simoom* was ready for dry-docking at Govan on 9 December. Her preliminary trials began on the 16th, with full power trials two days later. On 22nd she left for final trials, at the end of which she joined the Harwich Force. On 23 January 1917, in action with German destroyers off the Dutch coast, she was struck by a torpedo which killed 47 of her crew of 90. Still afloat but in poor condition, she was later sunk by the British destroyer *Nimrod*. (Author's collection)

While this book is concerned with events in the shipyard, at least a passing reference should be made to the wider social context that the yard and its people operated in during the war. While the Munitions of War Act sought to maximise production, it placed restrictions on trade unions by suspending the right to strike, stopping demarcation and introducing semi-skilled and unskilled workers to the factories and shipyards, a scheme known as dilution. Although the unions had agreed to these measures, there was nevertheless a simmering resentment against a background of rising prices and the justifiable suspicion that vast profits were being made out of war production. This led to considerable disruption, especially during 1915/16. At the same time, landlords made significant increases in rent, the reaction to which was a series of 'rent strikes', a situation eased when the Government passed the Rents Restrictions Act in December 1915 with rents frozen at 1914 levels for the duration of the war.

Above, right: Women 'dilutees' were drafted into the factories to replace men who had joined the forces. These women are carrying out semi-skilled work on capstan lathes, machining a variety of small components. The machines are driven by overhead line shafting. (UCS1-118-GEN-387-4)

Right: Their wartime-only status has been made abundantly clear by the handwritten comment behind them which says: 'When the boys come home we are not going to keep you any longer girls'. The women are testing condenser tubes under pressure. (UCS1-118-GEN-393-10)

Right: Two women tubing an oil cooler. (UCS1-118-GEN-387-3)

Right: Women working at high-speed engraving machines, engraving brass plates. (UCS1-118-GEN-387-6)

1917

KEEL LAYINGS

Wakeful	17 January
Watchman	17 January
War Thistle	2 March
War Hermit	12 March
Scimitar	30 May
Simoom (2)	2 July
Scout	25 October
Seabear	13 December

LAUNCHES

Skate	11 January
Tarpon	10 March
Ceres	24 March
Telemachus	21 April
Vanoc	14 June
Vanquisher	18 August
War Thistle	1 September
Wakeful	6 October
Watchman	1 December

COMPLETIONS

E50	23 January
Skate	19 February
Tarpon	26 April
Ceres	15 June
Telemachus	16 June
Vanoc	15 August
Vanquisher	2 October
War Thistle	9 October
Wakeful	16 November

Left: This was one of the photographer's favoured compositions, recording the moment when the completed ship, in this instance the dazzle-painted *Ormonde*, was manoeuvred out of the fitting-out basin. She was taken upriver to Meadowside Quay in Glasgow for provisioning. The date is 27 October 1917. (UCS1-118-425-28)

Above: The starboard triple expansion reciprocating engine for *Platypus* in the engine shops on 20 January 1917. From left to right: the small hand wheel on a horizontal plane at extreme left is the engine throttle valve, connected vertically to simple gears that regulated the amount of steam entering the engine through the inlet port. The large hand wheel to the right of that controlled the engine direction, either forward or astern, while the small steam engine beneath the wheel was a mechanised way of doing the same thing. On the middle column, the levers operate the engine drains and on the right-hand column the revolution counter can be seen. Finally, at bottom right, is the coupling to the thrust shaft and ultimately the propeller shaft. A direct drive turbine for the Orient liner *Ormonde* is in the background. (UCS1-118-432-2)

Left: Part of the vertical keel (with lightening holes) of *Hood* on 1 February 1917. The vertical keel is riveted to the outer flat keel which has been marked 'Hood'. The ship's steel stern casting was in several sections, the first part of which can be seen supported by the heavy timberwork sitting at the water's edge. On the casting by the top of this timberwork, the stubby horizontal projection is where the palm supporting the inner shaft bracket will be fitted. The stern casting, supported by an A frame and other timberwork, is being pulled into position by a chain attached to a screw or turnbuckle (inset, right) and although this may look crude, the frame will be exactly in position relative to the keel and ready for riveting. The stern casting was made by William Beardmore & Co Ltd at Parkhead, Glasgow. (Author's collection)

Left: On 21 October 1913 the Orient Steam Navigation Co's liner *Ormonde* was laid down at Clydebank, with an intended delivery date in late 1915. After the outbreak of war progress was slow, and in April 1915 the contract was suspended in favour of urgently required warships, not being restarted until May 1916, when work on *Repulse* began to tail off. She was requisitioned by the War Office for service as a troopship and is seen here on 10 February 1917, prior to her launch at 2.35pm that day. (UCS1-118-425-1)

Below: Launched on 10 March, *Tarpon* began a series of trials just one month later on 11 April, culminating with full power trials on 18 April. She left Clydebank for the last time on 26 April. The minelaying arrangements on the R class destroyers *Tarpon* and *Telemachus* were the subject of several photographs. This view of *Tarpon*, taken on 25 April 1917, shows the rails cantilevered over the ship's side on sponsons. A Type D depth charge sits on its cradle by the Carley Float. Ironically, *Tarpon* fell victim to a mine on 14 July 1917 off Dunkirk, although she was subsequently repaired. (UCS1-118-457-1)

130

Right: With built-up forecastle to support the flying-off platform and both hangars already fitted, *Pegasus* takes to the water on 9 June 1917. Laid down as the ferry *Stockholm* for the Great Eastern Railway Company on 21 May 1914, work on this vessel was slowed after the war began and labour directed to urgently required *Tiger* and *Barham*. She was launched bearing her original name on the bows. (UCS1-118-431-7)

Below and right: Two views of *Telemachus*, pictured on 15 June, show the minelaying rails from different vantage points. The view looking aft shows the complete system of rails from the davit used to mount the mines (adjacent to what looks like a torpedo warhead) to the stern. The Royal Mail liner *Ormonde* and the cruiser *Ceres*, which left Clydebank for the last time on this day, are in the background. (UCS1-118-458-3 and UCS1-118-458-4)

Right: In March 1917 the Company was asked by the Ministry of Munitions to make arrangement for the construction of 50 Mk IV tank hulls. Shipyard skills, principally platers and riveters, were well suited to manufacturing tanks of this type. From John Brown's, the hulls were sent to the Glasgow engineering firm Mirrlees Watson & Co Ltd, makers of sugar refining machinery in peacetime, for completion. The hulls were erected in the boiler shop, as seen here on 6 May with a number of Yarrow boilers at the far end. By the beginning of October, 27 hulls had been erected and forwarded to Mirrlees Watson. (UCS1-118-GEN-348-17)

Below: Workers gathering at one of the works' gates waiting for the hooter in June 1917. Stopping and starting times were strictly observed. (Author's collection)

Above and left: Ordered by the Australian Government in July 1914, work on *Platypus* proceeded very slowly and then came to complete stop until her future was decided. Commissioned on 25 March 1917 into the Royal Navy, *Platypus* is seen here leaving the fitting-out basin at Clydebank and then in the river on 30 April 1917. She was transferred to the Australian Navy in 1919 and not paid-off until 1956 and finally scrapped in Japan in 1958. (UCS1-118-432-14 and UCS1-118-432-16)

Right: Launched on 24 March, *Ceres* was all but complete by 31 May when she went to nearby Elderslie dry-dock for a hull inspection. Thereafter, she left Clydebank to run trials on 5 June, returning to the yard on 7 June. Undated, this and the following four photographs of *Ceres* were probably taken on 15 June, the day she left Clydebank for the last time. Note the large number of 6-inch shells lying on the quayside. (UCS1-118-459-22)

Below: The *Ceres* group of the C class was the first to mount two 6-inch guns forward of the bridge. This photograph shows this arrangement with the distinctive long blast screen to protect the forward mounting from the superfiring gun. Note the 6-inch shells stored immediately behind the breakwater and also around B gun. (UCS1-118-459-21)

Right: Note both pairs of twin torpedo tubes, and midships 6-inch gun with shell storage, and the group of shipyard officials in discussion with a naval officer by the port 3-inch gun. UCS1-118-459-23)

Right: The after part of *Ceres* showing the searchlight tower, the staggered port and starboard torpedo tubes and three 6-inch guns. (UCS1-118-459-20)

Below: Flying a barely visible White Ensign, *Ceres* leaves Clydebank to join the Fleet. UCS1-118-459-26

Above: *Pegasus*'s forward hangar for wheeled aircraft is visible with doors open in this view. Aircraft were wheeled out and raised to the flight deck by a rudimentary elevator. The forecastle has become rather crowded with capstan gear, winches and two 12pdr guns, one at either side. The bridge is being fitted with a semaphore telegraph, while a sailor works on the flag locker on the deck below. (UCS1-118-431-12)

Above: With little left to suggest a
ferry apart from the hull and its
distinctive rubbing strake, these
photographs show the hybrid carrier
Pegasus, in the final stages of fitting-out
on 17 August. (UCS1-118-431-9)

Below: The seaplane hangar and arrangement of cranes required to lower and recover seaplanes. Note the two 12pdr AA guns at the stern and on top of the hangar. (UCS1-118-431-17)

Above: The V class destroyer *Vanoc*'s
after twin 21-inch torpedo tubes
flanked by H Type mines – of which
she could carry 60. A rivet gang, with
the rivet boy standing by the rivet fire
with rivet tongs in hand, are carrying
out some last minute work by or on
the torpedo tubes. (UCS1-118-462-7)

Right: Fitted as a minelayer, *Vanoc*,
seen here leaving Clydebank on
15 August, was completed with her full
complement of torpedo tubes and
4-inch guns, although subsequently the
aftermost 4-inch gun and torpedo
tubes were removed to save weight.
(Author's collection)

Above: With merchant ship sinkings steadily rising throughout 1916/17, the Controller of Shipping placed an order with John Brown for two Standard ships, *War Thistle* and *War Hermit*, in January 1917. In total, five would be ordered. The counter stern and single propeller of *War Thistle*, a Type A dry cargo ship, is seen here in a dazzle camouflage scheme on the day of her launch, 1 September 1917.
(UCS1-118-468-6)

Right: Final touches applied to the troopship *Ormonde* on 24 October including a dazzle paint scheme. The notice on the gangway reads 'Smoking strictly prohibited on board this vessel at all times. Penalty instant dismissal.'
(UCS1-118-425-26)

Right: Midships view also taken on
24 October. Note the sail rigged on
one of the ship's lifeboats.
(UCS1-118-425-25)

Right: *Ormonde* in the river at
Clydebank on 13 November and about
to make the passage to Sydney where
she would begin duties as a troopship.
Her first voyage in this role was to take
troops of the Australian Imperial Force
to Port Said. After the war ended
Ormonde was involved in repatriating
Australian troops, and only after these
duties were completed was she able, in
November 1919, to began the
commercial service for which she was
laid own in October 1913.
(UCS1-118-425-31)

Above: Looking forward over a 4-inch gun and 'bandstand' to the two triple 21-inch torpedo tubes of the W class destroyer *Wakeful*, one of the first of her class to be completed. Seen here on 9 November 1917, *Wakeful* left Clydebank for the last time on 20 November. (UCS1-118-466-4)

Above: Looking towards *Hood*'s stern from the position of frame 270 on
12 December 1917. The hull has been built up to the level of the main deck with
only the quarterdeck above that, for which some of the frames are already in
position at the stern. Also seen at left is the framing for the bulge and the structure
of Y barbette. (Author's collection)

Above: *Train Ferry No 3* seen here on 3 November 1917 passing Clydebank. Built by Fairfield's at Govan, this ferry – along with two others built on the Tyne – was ordered by the War Office as part of the huge logistical operation supporting the British army in France. The ship's destination will be the military port of Richborough in Kent, for service to Calais and Dunkirk. She was subsequently named HMS *Daffodil*. (UCS1-118-OLD RED-340-4)

Right: This undated photo shows the troopship *Missanabie* sailing past Clydebank, heading for Glasgow packed with troops. Men have crowded to the side of the ship causing her to list slightly as they look at the shipyard and *Hood* on slipway No 3. Built by Barclay Curle & Co for Canadian Pacific Railways, the ship was requisitioned and converted for troopship duties in 1915. According to Canadian sources, *Missanabie* visited Glasgow once as a troopship, departing St Johns on 19 December and arriving in Glasgow on 31 December 1917, the likely date of this photograph, carrying elements of No 9 Siege Battery. *Missanabie* was torpedoed and sunk on 9 September 1918 by *U87*. (UCS1-118-GEN-325-2)

1918

KEEL LAYINGS

Scythe	4 January
Seafire	27 February
Searcher	30 March
War Crane	18 April
Seawolf	30 April
Verity	17 May
Venomous	31 May
Enterprise	26 June
Veteran	30 August
Bata	19 December

LAUNCHES

Simoom	26 January
Scimitar	27 February
War Hermit	28 March
Scotsman	30 March
Scout	27 April
Scythe	25 May
Seabear	6 July
Seafire	10 August
Hood	22 August
Searcher	11 September
Seawolf	2 November
Venomous	21 December

COMPLETIONS

Watchman	26 January
Simoom	12 March
War Hermit	29 March
Scimitar	29 April
Scotsman	21 May
Scout	15 June
Scythe	8 July
Seabear	7 September
Seafire	24 October
Searcher	25 November

Left: *Scimitar* on 11 April, the day after she completed full power trials. She left to join the fleet on 13 April. On the other side of the basin the K class submarine *K7* is undergoing a brief refit after arriving at Clydebank on 5 April. Her bows have already been marked off by platers, ready to receive the 'swan' forecastle. (UCS1-118-473-2)

Left: *Hood* on 17 February 1918 looking forward along the starboard side in the vicinity of frame 239 (slightly forward of the main mast) and by number '28 S^D' 12-inch side armour plate. The man looking at the camera, who happens to be holding a brush and pan set (!), is standing in an upper bulge compartment. At the bottom left, a plate from the next strake of plating has been bolted temporarily in place. All visible rivet holes on the plate line up with those on the frame and plate underneath, except the one circled in chalk on the frame itself which will require drilling and reaming before riveting can take place. Note the numerous butt straps on the side plating. (UCS1-118-460-407)

Below left and below: In October the Admiralty asked John Brown & Co to carry out the first refit of the submarine *K2*, which had been completed in May 1917 at HM Dockyard Portsmouth. This was not Clydebank's first involvement with *K2* as her Brown–Curtis turbines, and those of *K1*, were manufactured by the Company. *K2* arrived at Clydebank on 26 November 1917 and by the time the two views here were taken, on 11 February 1918, much of the work had been completed. The refit included the fitting of 'swan bows' over the existing bows, removal of twin torpedo tubes in the superstructure and the reduction of guns from three to two and the repositioning of one of these to make two on top of the superstructure. Note the torpedo derrick behind the conning tower, the forward 4-inch gun and the after 3-inch HA gun aft of this. (UCS1/118/GEN/326/7 and UCS1/118/GEN/326/8)

Three details of *Simoom*, not to be confused with the earlier destroyer of the same name built at Clydebank, taken on 11 March 1918, the day before she left the yard.

Below: Bridge from port side. (UCS1-118-472-7)

Above: This midships view shows a
4-inch gun on its 'bandstand' with
three John Brown workers, including a
woman 'dilutee'. A fourth person on
the ladderway appears as a ghostly
figure in this time exposure. *War Hermit*
is in the background. (UCS1-118-472-5)

Below: The refinement of depth charging gear that took place over the war years did nothing to reduce the clutter of equipment at the stern. Further forward the searchlight is being tested. (UCS1-118-472-4)

Right: *Hood*'s port side on 13 March looking forward from the vicinity of frame 255–275 (close to where the mainmast, port engine room and torpedo control tower will be). Although plating of the ship's side, including the bulge, is well underway, most of the plates are fixed to the frames and to one another using bolts – approximately six bolts per plate. Once sufficient plates have been 'screwed-up', riveters take over, driving many thousands of rivets for the section of hull seen here. Note the rudimentary wooden staging with no guardrails or protection of any description. Given the height from the ground and intense noise in the working environment, a moment's loss of concentration could be fatal. (Author's collection)

Right: The Red Star liner *Lapland*, built by Harland & Wolff at Belfast in 1909, passing John Brown's on 15 March 1918 in service as a troopship. (UCS1-118-GEN-257-5)

Three views of the S class
destroyer *Scimitar*, pendant
number G41, taken on
11 April 1918.

Right: *Scimitar*'s after 4-inch mounting
on its bandstand. The two men working
at the stern appear to be securing a
D Type depth charge. (UCS1-118-473-5)

Left: The fore funnel and bridge.
(UCS1-118-473-6)

Below: Test-firing a 21-inch torpedo in the fitting-out basin. A wire attached to the torpedo will ensure it has a very short run. This photograph was taken on 26 April 1918. (UCS1-118-473-10)

Above: The second of Clydebank's Standard ships, *War Hermit,* a Type AO tanker, was launched on 28 March and completed in less than two months. This view looking forward towards the bridge, taken on 25 April, shows the simple nature of her design. The notice board beside the two men looking at the camera is the standard one for tankers – about no smoking 'except in such places as are appointed by the Captain'. The small deckhouse immediately above this notice has a small nameplate above the door saying 'Smoking Room'. (UCS1-118-469-4)

Right: Assisted by the paddle tug *Flying Scotsman, War Hermit* slips her moorings in John Brown's fitting-out basin at 12.45pm on 26 April 1918, and prepares to head up river to Glasgow. (UCS1-118-469-8)

Right: Two S class destroyers, *Scotsman* and *Scout*, on 8 May 1918. Note the distinctive turtleback forecastle, which has been cut back abruptly to allow the torpedo tubes on either side of the bridge to train. (Author's collection)

Below: Lieutenant General Jan Christian Smuts, soldier, statesman and a member of
the British Imperial War Cabinet, addressing workers in the shipyard on 17 May
1918. Headgear indicated status in shipyards and here most of the crowd are wearing
cloth bunnets, standard wear for working men. Soft hats indicate technical staff such
as draughtsmen, while shipyard managers wore bowler hats. A handful of women are
present, as are service personnel. (UCS1-118-GEN-397-3)

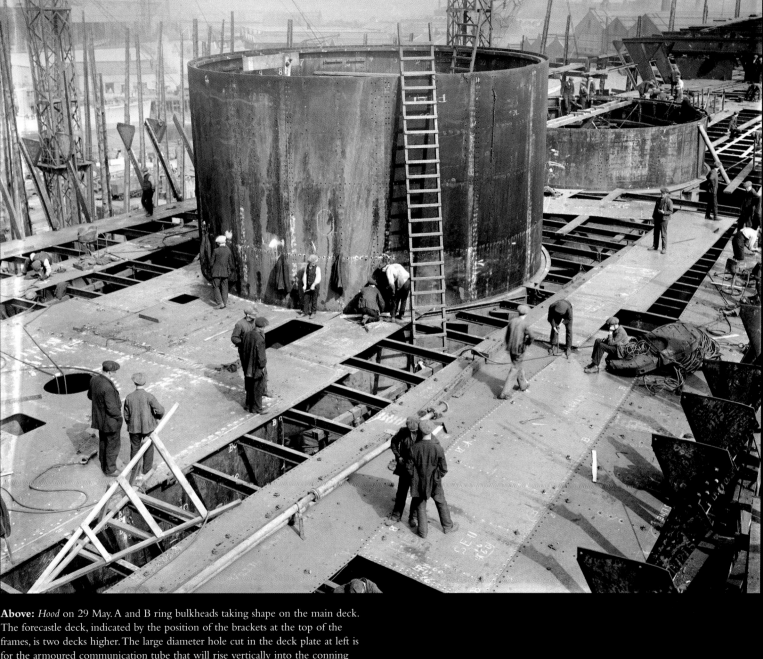

Above: *Hood* on 29 May. A and B ring bulkheads taking shape on the main deck.
The forecastle deck, indicated by the position of the brackets at the top of the
frames, is two decks higher. The large diameter hole cut in the deck plate at left is
for the armoured communication tube that will rise vertically into the conning
tower. The two men at bottom middle are unusually close together because they are
trying to be heard over the noise of pneumatic riveting. Numerous air-lines for
pneumatic riveting guns are lying around. (Author's collection)

Right: A magnificent photograph of the fitting-out basin taken on 5 June 1918, encompassing much of what the shipyard was about during the latter stages of the war. The photographer has positioned himself on the lower part of the 150-ton derrick crane and captured, nearest to the camera, the stern of minelaying destroyer *Vanquisher* and the Standard ship *War Thistle* with her screw thrashing the water during a basin trial. On the other side of the basin, the Orient liner *Ormonde* is lying fitted out as a troopship with a then–ubiquitous Clyde puffer alongside. Note the seamen's kit bags under the dockside crane, the torpedo warheads in crates behind the sailors and the mines at bottom right. (UCS1-118-GEN-342-1)

Below: A model of the cruiser *Ceres* made in the Clydebank model shop photographed on 9 July 1918, by which time the ship had been completed for a year. The shipyard made many models of the ships it built and commissioned others from well-known modelmakers such as Bassett Lowke. (UCS1-118-459-29)

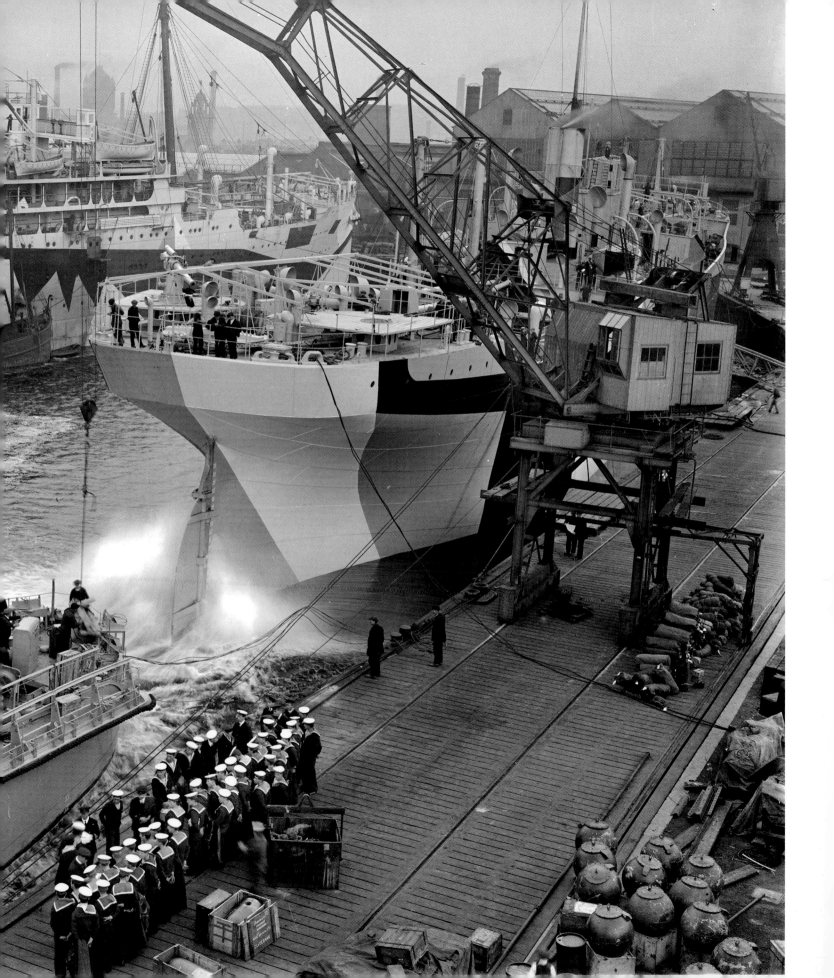

Right: The West Yard on 5 June 1918 showing six building slips, all of which are occupied with the last of the war programme destroyers. *Seawolf*, in frame, is nearest the camera with, from right to left, *Seabear*, *Searcher*, *Venomous*, *Seawolf* and *Verity*. Compare this photograph to the one of the West Yard on page 54 taken four years earlier. The covered shipbuilding gantry has been extended to cover four berths while the two berths nearest the camera have been equipped with the latest type of shipbuilding tower cranes capable of lifting 12 tons. The cost of rebuilding the West Yard, approved by the Admiralty, had reached £46,229 by September 1919, of which the company claimed £18,491 as a grant. (UCS1-118-GEN-337-2)

Below: *Scout* leaving Clydebank on 14 June 1918. She is flying her pendant number G35. (UCS1-118-475-1)

Below: Watched by comparatively few people in the yard and on the opposite bank, *Hood* is launched into the Clyde on 22 August 1918. Under normal circumstances the launch of the world's largest warship would have attracted many tens of thousands of people. (UCS1-118-460-346)

Below: *Scythe* in the final stages of
fitting out on 19 June. Heavy barbette
armour for *Hood* is lying on the
quayside. (UCS1-118-476-2)

Bottom: *Scythe* departing Clydebank
on 5 July 1918. (UCS1-118-476-3)

Below: This view of John Brown's East Yard was taken from the forecastle of *Hood* on 21 August, the day before she was launched. The roof of the plater's shed is at left; at the end of this is the smithy with two chimneys. The Standard ship *War Rider* is in frame on No 1 berth, while one of *Pegasus*'s seaplane cranes is lying on the ground forward of *War Rider*. Rothesay Dock, full of dazzle-painted merchant ships and colliers, lies beyond the shipyard. (UCS1-118-GEN-322-4)

Right: *Seabear* running trials in August 1918. (UCS1-118-477-2)

Above: *Hood* photographed on 4 September 1918, just over two weeks after her launch. An auxiliary steam engine is being lowered into the machinery space, guided by men pulling on wire ropes. At bottom left, the vertical plating being erected is marked 'Stage Wanted here', indicating a position for wooden planking, or that staging is to be put there. At right, the anti-torpedo bulges are still to be completed and faired into the ship's side. The destroyer is probably the S class *Seafire* launched on 10 August. Although quite a few men are evident in this photograph, it does not convey the actuality of events as employment returns for *Hood* on this day record 2114 persons employed exclusively on this ship. Of these, 1052 were journeymen, 273 apprentices, 550 'helpers' and 215 were boys. An additional 24 helpers were women. (No catalogue number)

Right: In the early years of the war, pneumatic riveting machines were gradually introduced as a means of speeding production and using fewer men. These machines were heavy and in this trial on shell plating photographed on 6 October 1918, out-rigging gear is being used to take the weight of the gun, requiring the riveter to provide forward pressure only and work the trigger. The supporting bracket was bolted to the plate using a rivet hole. Thereafter the riveter would have been able to reach a number of rivet holes using the slide mechanism before the bracket required to be repositioned. (UCS1-118-470-3)

Left: According to the negative register, this is a wartime propaganda meeting held by Captain George Barley. However, a French officer is addressing the crowd. (UCS1-118-GEN-301-2)

POST-WAR

Vessels begun during WWI but completed after

LAUNCHES	
Verity	19 March 1919
Veteran	26 April 1919
War Crane	3 June 1919
Bata	10 September 1919
Enterprise	23 December 1919

COMPLETIONS	
Seawolf	28 January 1919
Venomous	– June1919
War Crane	2 July 1919
Verity	17 September 1919
Veteran	12 November 1919
Bata	14 October 1919
Hood	9 January 1920★
Enterprise	9 April 1920★★

★ Date of departure from Clydebank. Taken to Rosyth for completion. Commissioned 15 May 1920.

★★ Date of departure from Clydebank. Taken to Devonport for completion. Commissioned 7 April 1926.

Left: *Enterprise*, 11 December 1919. Laid down on 28 June 1918, the E class cruiser *Enterprise* was destined for a brief career at Clydebank. The end of the war on 11 November 1918 brought with it cancellations for many warships recently ordered or in the early stages of construction. *Enterprise* and her sister *Emerald* (building on the Tyne) were lucky to escape cancellation. Fitted with Brown-Curtis turbines of 80,000 shp, she is seen here, minus propellers, on 11 December, a few weeks before her launch on 23 December. After launching she was towed to Devonport for leisurely fitting-out and was not completed until April 1926. (UCS1/118/484/18)

Veteran, a Modified W class destroyer, was the last of the wartime destroyers completed at Clydebank and, apart from *Hood*, the last of the wartime construction programme. She is seen here in four photographs taken on 7 November 1919.

Below: *Veteran*'s fore funnel and bridge photographed between two of *Hood*'s 5.5-inch guns. The Great Eastern Railway Co's cross-channel ferry *Antwerp*, launched on 25 November, is lying on the other side of the basin. (UCS1-118-485-15)

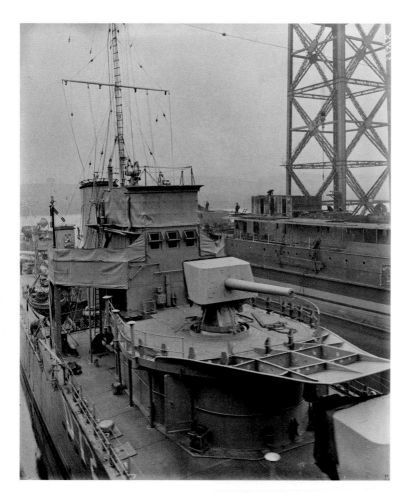

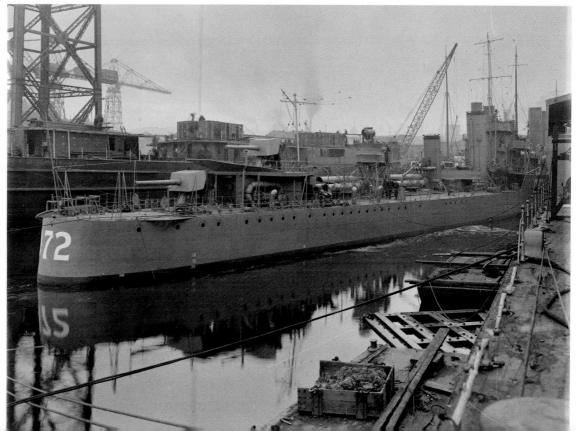

Above: The bridge and forward superfiring 4.7-inch gun. (UCS1-118-485-17)

Above, right: Detail of the gyro and searchlight platform, the after triple 21-inch torpedo tubes and the depth charge thrower. (UCS1-118-485-12)

Right: This view of *Veteran* taken from *Hood*'s quarterdeck shows how low the battlecruiser was aft in the water. (UCS1-118-485-18)

Right: When *Hood* left Clydebank on
9 January 1920 it was to go to Rosyth
where the final stages of fitting-out
were completed, including dry-docking
and fitting the revolving hood and
15-inch rangefinder on the control top.
On completion, she returned to the
Firth of Clyde to finalise contractor's
trials. She is seen here in this striking
silhouette, with more than a touch of
Götterdämmerung about it, running at
high speed into rough seas on the
measured mile off Arran. On the
successful completion of trials, she
returned to Rosyth and was
commissioned on 15 May 1920.
(UCS1-118-460-500)

Below: War is over. Taken on 2 July 1920 as two schoolboys watch, the intermediate liner *Montcalm* is prepared for her launch, which was on the following day. Laid down on 10 January 1919 for Canadian Pacific, she was John Brown's first merchantman since the end of the war. (UCS1-118-464-7)

Right: Canadian Pacific and John Brown management with invited guests form the launch party on the platform draped with the flags of friendly nations. *Montcalm*'s sponsor was Lady Fisher, wife of Canadian Pacific's General Manager, seen here at right of the Union Jack having just launched the ship. Sir Thomas Bell, Clydebank's Managing Director, stands behind her and to the left, distinguished by his spectacles and moustache. (UCS1-118-464-10)

Right: *Montcalm* pictured on 2 December 1921 in the fitting-out basin. Her maiden voyage from Liverpool to Canada was on 17 January 1922. (UCS1-118-464-14)

Appendix 1: SHIPYARD DIARY

The following shipyard chronology is an edited compilation from three Company sources: the Directors' Minute Books,[1] Monthly Shipyard Reports[2] and the Shipyard Diary.[3]

1914

Month	Date	Comment
August	15	**In consequence of acceleration of work on war vessels under construction, a special service of trains was arranged for Saturday evenings and Sundays by Caledonian Railway Co until further notice.**
	26	**Minutes.** Thomas Bell reports on action to be taken to accelerate warship work noting that good progress has been made on *Tiger* and three TBDs. Armstrong's have paid an instalment on *Almirante Latorre* but third instalment is two months overdue. Agreed to start a War Relief Fund amongst workmen and officials.
September	1	**Report.** Order from Admiralty on 31 July to expedite completion of *Tiger* by means of employing every available man on her and working continuously with overtime, night shifts and Sunday. The acceleration of work on *Tiger* and 3 TBDs progressing well.
	23	**Minutes.** Letter from Armstrong's saying that *Almirante Latorre* to be transferred to RN. Acceleration of work on Tiger and 3 TBDs progressing well.
	28	**Report.** Stock destroyers No 429 [*Medea*] and No 430 [*Medusa*] ordered. Men borrowed to work on *Tiger* have now been returned to *Barham*. Works closed for Autumn Holiday but workmen employed on war vessels requested to attend as usual.
October	4	*Tiger* left Clydebank on Sunday [4 October] for Portsmouth.
	5	*Milne* launched.
	21	**Minutes.** Tender for HMS *Canterbury* accepted. First Russian battleship *Sevastopol* running experimental steam trials.
	27	*Barham* to be accelerated for completion in mid-summer 1915.
November	19	*Morris* launched.
	24	**Minutes.** Thomas Bell has met with the Navy Board to discuss building submarine hulls, more TBDs and the acceleration of other work. Tender to Admiralty for construction of diesel engines for submarines on basis of cost plus percentages for charges and profit. Subscription for Clydebank Belgian Relief Fund amounted to £243. The Company agreed to put in £100.
December	31	*Barham* launched at 12 noon. To enable men to watch the launch, work was stopped at 11.30.
		Minutes. Orders for two destroyers No 439 *Mameluke* and 440 *Ossory* and 3 submarines 436/7/8 received. Licence from Vickers to manufacture submarine diesel engines.

1915

Month	Date	Comment
January	17	*Barham* moved along dock wall to ship foremast.
	20	**Minutes.** Thomas Bell has met with Admiralty officials and Mr McGowan of Palmer's to discuss the transfer of HMS *Repulse* to Clydebank.
	21	*Barham* moved along dock wall to ship turbines.
	23	*Barham* moved along dock wall to ship barbette armour.
	26	**Report.** *Barham* to be given precedence for 15-inch guns and mountings.
	30	*Medea* launched.
	26	To be given precedence for delivery of 15-inch guns and mountings for *Barham*.
February	17	*Moorsom* left for final trial.
	22	**Minutes.** Agreed that designs of TBDs to be made by us and that subs by either Vickers or Armstrong's.
	23	**Report.** Black Sea battleships – consignments of valves and pipes being despatched almost weekly to Russia. Regret to report that although a mutual recommendation on behalf of the executive of the Masters [employers] and the Men was adopted and signed at York on 12 February agreeing to an increase of 3 shillings, 4 pence and one farthing per week to all engineers and machinemen, the men went out on strike on 18 inst. without a ballot and notification to the Masters. [There was considerable unrest among engineers and shipbuilding workers, especially on Clydeside, because of rises in the cost of living. The men returned to work for 4 shillings per week].
	24	SS *Aydon* arrived from Barrow with gun mountings for *Barham* [Y mounting].
March	12	SS *Aydon* arrived from Barrow with gun mountings for *Barham* [X mounting].
	27	*Medusa* launched.
	29	**Minutes.** Two more TBDs ordered on cost plus basis N°444 *Napier* and 445 *Narbrough*. Received a sub-contract from Wallsend Slipway for half set of turbines for large cruiser [*Furious*].
April	14	SS *Aydon* arrived with gun mountings for *Prince Rupert*.
	27	**Report.** Work on *Ormonde*, *Stockholm* and *Platypus* suspended as men are needed for Admiralty contracts. Our definite price for the half set of turbines for this vessel has been accepted by Wallsend Slipway. Order to be completed in 9 to 10 months.

May	1	*Mons* launched.
	27	**Minutes**. Prices given to Coventry Syndicate for Greek cruisers and destroyers. Two more TBDs ordered No 447 and 448 [*Penn* and *Peregrine*]. Designs for new Spanish naval programme well under way.
		Report. Ship 425 Hellenic destroyer *Kriti* now *Medea* and *Lesvos* now *Medusa*. King George V visited the works on 17 May.
	29	*Marne* launched.
June	4 & 14	SS *Aydon* arrived with mountings for *Barham* [A and B mountings].
	23	**Minutes**. Spanish plans being arranged and adjusted with other members of Coventry Syndicate.
	24	*Medea* leaves yard for final trial.
	29	**Report**. Order from Kawasaki Dockyard & Co Ltd for cruising turbines and gearing for battleship building in Japan [probably for *Ise* building at Kobe]. Lord Fisher visited works on 18 June to see progress on *Repulse* and appeared very much impressed with progress that has been made.
July	1	*Medusa* leaves yard for final trial.
	15	Works closed for Fair Holiday. [The name given on Clydeside to the annual summer holiday.]
	21	Works reopened in accordance with Admiralty notice.
	26	**Minutes**. Letter from Ministry of Munitions intimating that from 12 July 1915, Clydebank would be a Controlled Establishment. [This refers to the passing of the Munitions of War Act in July 1915.]
	27	**Report**. HMS *Canada*: final dock trials completed 29 June. [Brown-Curtis turbines supplied to Armstrong Whitworth]. *Barham* completed on contract viz 15 July, but armament manufacturers [Vickers] have not completed forward mountings. *Mons* completed one month ahead of contract in July.
August	3	Unrest among large numbers of skilled workers for increase in War Allowance.
	14	*Mameluke* launched.
	18	*Barham* commissioned in the dock at Clydebank.
	26	*Barham* leaves yard for Tail of the Bank.[4]
September	2	On trials, *Barham* developed over 77,000 shp and made 25.51 knots.
	27	*Marne* handed over at TOB.
October	4	Gun trials of *Barham* carried out. Sole damage throughout ship was 9 earthenware fittings in some lavatories.
	27	**Minutes**. Tender for machinery for K class flotilla leader building at Portsmouth accepted.
	30	*Mameluke* left yard for final trial.
November	27	*Napier* launched.
December	2	Thanks to excellent progress made on hull and also exceptionally quick delivery of huge propeller and stern tube shafts from Atlas Works at Sheffield, *Repulse* will be ready for launch 9 months from actually commencing work on building slip.
	4	*Ossory* left yard for final trial.
	21	**Report**. Order for two further TBDs No 455 and 456 [*Simoom* was No 455 and *Windsor Castle* No 456. This probably refers to *Tarpon* which was No 457]. It is hoped to work 12 plates of 6-inch armour belt on either side of *Repulse* over the next ten days. *Canterbury* launched at 12.20 by Miss Lascelles.
	31	Works closed at 12 noon for New Year Holiday.

1916

Month	Date	Comment
January	5	Works reopened.
	8	*Repulse* launched.
	22	*Napier* leaves yard for final trial.
	26	**Report**. First HP turbine for *Furious* tested on 22 and 24 January. Repairs to machinery of *Mameluke* completed.
March	2	**Minutes**. Russian machinery to be sent via Archangel [for Russian battleship *Imperator Alexandr III*]. *Narbrough* launched.
		Report. Both HP turbines and one LP turbine have been steam balanced and run in the shop and the last LP turbine will be ready for steaming next week [*Repulse*]. *P33* machinery ready to go to Napier and Millers yard at Old Kilpatrick.
April	2	SS *Rosehill* arrived with 15-inch turntables for *Repulse*.
		SS *Wolhandel* arrived to load machinery [for Russian battleship *Imperator Aleksandr III*].
	8	*Penn* launched.
	21	Notification from Admiralty that they wished us to prepare for the construction of a vessel similar to *Repulse* for which we would shortly receive drawings and particulars, but not urgent in nature.[5]
	28	SS *Rosehill* arrived with 15-inch turntables for *Repulse*.
	29	*Narbrough* leaves yard for final trial.
May	3	**Minutes**. Notification from Admiralty about a ship similar to *Repulse*. To prepare for this ship with drawings and particulars to be received shortly.
	4	Owing to ground giving way, the attempted launch of submarine *E35* on 22 April was not successful and the vessel slid sideways carrying the launch ways with her.[6]

Elswick cruiser turbines [for *Furious*] now completed and delivered safely to Newcastle upon Tyne.

June   1   **Report**. Amalgamated Society of Engineers are taking a determined attitude regarding increase in wages.

As *Repulse* completes, work on *Ormonde* and *Platypus* has again commenced.

Lord Pirrie has arranged with the Chairman of Union Castle to place an order for a large passenger vessel of 655ft oa, the duplicate of one building at Belfast.

July   1   *Rowena* launched.

    12   *Peregrine* leaves yard.

    14   Ship 460, informed of ship's name by letter today [*Hood*].

    24   *E35* leaves yard.

    25   **Minutes**. Admiralty to pay a fixed price for *K1*'s machinery. This was originally to have been on a time and percentage basis.

Accepted a fixed price for TBDs 449 to 452 [*Romola, Rowena, Restless, Rigorous*].

Letter from Harland & Wolff about steamships for Union Castle and Glen Lines.

    25   **Report**. Unrest among a large number of skilled workers for increase in war allowance continues as also agitation to get holidays in relays. [There had been considerable industrial unrest on Clydeside in 1916 over several grievances.]

Contract for SS *Stockholm*, Ship 431 [*Pegasus*] has been stopped. K class turbines, 453 and 454 [turbine order placed for submarines *K1* and *K2*].

    29   Works visited by an international group of journalists.

August   8   *Repulse* commissioned in Clydebank Dock.

    12   *Restless* launched.

    14   *Repulse* leaves yard for TOB.

    17   *Romola* leaves yard for final trial.

    30   **Minutes**. Two further TBDs ordered 462 and 463 [*Vanoc* and *Vanquisher*].

    31   **Report**. *Repulse* commissioned in Clydebank Dock on 8 August. On preliminary trials on the Firth of Clyde engines were worked up to 106,000 shp without a hitch. Official steam trials and gun trials were on Tuesday 15th giving every satisfaction as regards speed, power and stiffness. While official time for construction from date of laying keel is 18.5 months it is only fair to say that the official date for laying the keel, 25 January 1915, was a paper date only to enable some official to wire Lord Fisher that it had been laid on his birthday. The designs were not sufficiently advanced nor was enough material in the yard to proceed with the work for another six weeks and even then it was with the greatest difficulty that working drawings could be prepared and approved to keep pace with the ship's construction.

September 5   First Lord and Third Sea Lord visit Clydebank to see progress [Arthur Balfour and Rear Admiral Frederick Charles Tudor].

    16   *E36* launched.

    26   **Report**. *Rowena* is fifteenth destroyer handed over since start of war. Asked by Admiralty to complete *Ceres* in one year. We agree that this is possible but only if engines fitted on berth.

    29   *Rowena* leaves yard for final trial.

    30   *Rigorous* launched.

October   21   *Restless* leaves yard for final trial.

    28   *Platypus* launched

November 2   **Report**. Admiralty most seriously continue to impress on us the importance of dilution and of employing as many women as possible. Whilst we have been able to effect considerable dilution in the manning of smaller machines in Engine Shops and in deploying clerks in the Counting House, it has not been easy to effect dilution in the shipyard. We have started in the Joiners Shop and hope to have several women in Plumbers Shop, Sheet Iron Shop and Sawmill. *Hood*: sufficient information is gradually being obtained from the Admiralty to enable more material to be ordered for this vessel and to employ a few more men on her construction, but in view of the alterations in her design, comparatively slow progress can only be made until the beginning of next year.

Fitting turbines to *K2* at Govan Dry Dock.

Agreements for manufacture of Brown-Curtis turbines made with: David Rowan, Barclay Curle and Swan Hunter & Wigham Richardson.

    13   *E50* launched.

    23   *E36* leaves yard.

    30   **Report**. We are taking over completion of *P33* due to slow progress in Glasgow Harbour. This as a result of request by Admiralty made at end of October. Manufacturing boilers for *P42, P43* and *P64*.

Rigorous leaves yard.

December 13   *Obedient* arrives in yard for slight repair.

    21   **Minutes**. Proposals for building Chinese coast defence battleships in conjunction with Palmers sent to R Backhouse. Orders for two V class TBDs 466 and 467 [*Wakeful* and *Watchman*].

Report. Machinery for *Almirante Cochrane* suspended [battleship building at Armstrong's].

Turbine parts for *Tormentor* building at Stephen's transferred from Beardmore's as they are too busy.

22 *Simoom* left yard for final trial.

24 *Obedient* left yard.

1917

Month	Date	Comment

January | 11 | *Skate* launched.

22 *E50* left yard for final trial.

February | 1 | **Minutes**. Controller of Merchant Shipping has placed an order for two standard ships 468 *War Thistle* and 469 *War Hermit* and for hull and boilers for one more, 470 *War Rider*. Fullarton Hodgart and Barclay making engines for third ship. Lord Pirrie has suggested laying down a fourth ship, *War Crane,* on No 7 berth and the Shipping Controller has gladly accepted.
Letter from Russian Shipbuilding Co for designs for Brown-Curtis turbines for four destroyers.

10 *Ormonde* launched.

19 *Skate* left yard.

March | 1 | **Minutes**. Ministry of Munitions have asked us to make arrangements for construction of 50 Mark IV tank hulls.
Report. *Hood* to be pushed with all despatch.

10 *Tarpon* launched.

24 **Minutes**. Representative of the Russian Shipbuilding Co arrived in connection with designs for twin-screw turbine machinery for submarines.
Ceres launched.

29 Have received major alterations to *Stockholm* from Admiralty.

30 *Platypus* left yard for trial.

April | 21 | *Telemachus* launched.

25 **Minutes**. Orders for two Improved R class TBDs and from H&W for 5 sets of boilers for standard ships.

26 **Report**. On 17 April received orders for 4 destroyers of improved R class 472 to 475 [*Simoom, Scimitar, Scotsman, Scout*].
Orders also received for 5 sets of boilers for standard ships from Harland & Wolff.
Tarpon left yard.

June | 7 | Both North British Diesel and Vickers have taken licences for Brown-Curtis turbines.
Order for engines for SS *Nariva* building at Stephens.

5 Letter from Admiralty about purchase of *Stockholm* from Great Eastern Railway Co.

9 *Stockholm* launched.

14 *Vanoc* launched.

15 *Ceres* left for TOB.

16 *Telemachus* leaves yard.

22 **Report**. Letter from Admiralty saying they will purchase *Stockholm* outright from Great Eastern Railway Co. Mark IV machines – nine hulls completed and sent away at the end of May to be completed by Mirrlees Watson & Co. We could complete 5 per week if we were allowed to despatch them. Satisfactory progress on *Hood* but more men would help progress of hull.

28 **Report**. Two days ago all shipyard riveters stopped work in Clyde district over wages. The matter is in the hands of the Ministry of Munitions in London.

July | 12 | Works closed for Fair Holiday.

24 Works reopened.

August | 2 | **Minutes**. Orders for 5 further TBDs 476 to 480 [*Scythe, Seabear, Seafire, Searcher* and *Seawolf*] and also the machinery for a TBD building at Denny [No 481 *Sesame*].
Report. During last week in June, riveters working on standard ships stopped work on the Clyde as they were not highly paid enough. They returned on 2 July as the matter went to arbitration. 17 Mark IV tanks completed and 13 despatched.

15 *Vanoc* left yard.

18 *Vanquisher* launched.

21 *Pegasus* leaves yard for trials.

September | 1 | *War Thistle* launched.

October | 2 | *Vanquisher* leaves yard.

6 *Wakeful* launched.

9 *War Thistle* leaves yard.

27 *K2* arrives in yard.

November | 1 | We have been requested by Admiralty to undertake first refit of *K2*.

2 *Ormonde* leaves yard.

20 *Wakeful* leaves yard.

29 **Minutes**. Orders from deputy Controller of Auxiliary Shipping to complete fitting machinery to SS *Ardgoil* and to complete machining of machinery for *Rhode Island*. To be sent to Clydebank for completion.

December   2   *Watchman* launched.

1918
Month Date Comment

January   22   **Minutes**. Orders for two TBDs of V class 482 [*Venomous*] and 483 [*Verity*]. Admiralty request that the West Yard be improved. Grant in aid and allowances for deductions from Excess Profits will cover 40% of cost. A spend of £50,000 anticipated including extension to plater's shed and covered berth as well as two jib cranes for No 1 berth.

            26   *Watchman* left yard.
                 Simoom launched.

            31   **Report**. Orders for 4 boilers for Harland & Wolff. Letter of 22 January 1918 regarding extension for shipyard and extending covered berths in West Yard.

February   27   *Scimitar* launched.

March   12   *Simoom* leaves yard.

            20   **Minutes**. Order for E class cruiser and six further TBDs [*Enterprise, Veteran, Vigo, Wistful, Virulent, Volage, Volcano*].

            28   *War Hermit* launched.

            30   *Scotsman* launched.

April   5   *K7* arrived in yard.

            13   *Scimitar* left yard.

            26   *War Hermit* left yard.

            27   *Scout* launched.

May   2   **Minutes**. Agreement with Cunard for reserving berths for a period of time. Negotiations with Orient Line in progress.

            21   *Scotsman* left yard.

            25   *Scythe* launched.

June   15   *Scout* leaves yard.

July   1   *K7* left yard.

             8   *Scythe* left yard for TOB.
                 Seabear launched.

            10   SS *Hebburn* arrived to load machinery for Newcastle [No 423 *Almirante Cochrane*].

August   1   **Minutes**. Order from Controller General of Merchant Shipping for one set of standard ship machinery to replace set given to East Coast yard.

            10   *Seafire* launched.

            14   Barge with one paddle tug arrived to load batteries for *K8*. *K8* arrives in yard.

            15   Lighter *Vulcan* arrived to load torpedoes from *K8*.

            22   *Hood* launched.

            24   HMS *Lightfoot* arrived to receive turbines.

September   7   *Seabear* left yard.

            11   *Searcher* launched.

         12/16   *Hood* moved to ship barbette armour.

            26   *Scout* returned to yard to have boiler repaired.

October   24   *Seafire* left yard.
                 K8 left yard for TOB.

November   2   *Seawolf* launched.

            11   Armistice between Allies and Germany signed. Yard stopped about 11am and resumed on Wednesday 13th at 9.45 but the start was only moderate.

            13   Lighter *Westernlight* arrived to load stem casting of *Repulse* for conveyance to Rosyth.

            25   *Searcher* left yard.

            28   **Minutes**. Order for another standard ship of B type received ship No 491 [*Bata*].

December   9   *Scout* left yard.

            16   *War Rider* launched.

            18   **Minutes**. Order for two ships for G E Railway Co received.

            21   *Venom* launched.

NOTES
1 UCS 1/1/1.
2 Uncatalogued Managers Monthly Reports, held at Sheffield Archives, Sheffield.
3 UCS 1/10/2.
4 The Firth of Clyde is often referred to as the 'Tail of the Bank'.

5 This is the first reference to the battlecruiser *Hood*.
6 Despite their undoubted prowess as shipbuilders, *E36* quite literally slipped away. The submarine fell off the slipway ending up on her starboard side on the ground. Repairs took over four months.

Appendix 2: SHIPS BUILT OR UNDER CONSTRUCTION 1914-1919

No	Name	Owner	Keel - Launch - Completion	Basic Particulars	Fate
409	Aquitania	Cunard SS Co Ltd	5/6/11 - 21/4/13 - 18/5/14	901' x 97' x 49'7" x 45,647gt Turbines 62,000shp 23.35k	Scrapped Metal Industries, Faslane 21/2/1950
418	Tiger	Admiralty	20/6/12 - 15/12/13 - 3/10/14	704' x 90.5' x 44'3" 35,000 disp. Turbines (BC) 108,000shp, 29k	Scrapped Ward, Inverkeithing 1932
		Battlecruiser		8 - 13.5". 12 - 6", 2 - 3", 5mgs,10 Lewis, 4 - 21"TT	
421		Russian Government	Machinery for Russian battleship **Imperatritsa Mariya** building at Russud Yard, Nikolaev. Turbines (BC) 26,500shp 21k		
422		Russian Government	Machinery for Russian battleship **Imperator Alexandr III** building at - as above. Later *Volya* and *General Alekseyev*		
423		Chilean Government	Machinery for battleship **Almirante Cochrane** (originally called *Santiago*) building by Armstrong Whitworth. Geared turbines (BC) 50,000 shp 24k		
424	Barham	Admiralty	24/2/13 - 31/12/14 - 10/15	634'6" x 90'6" x 44'9" x 31,100disp. Turbines (BC) 76,575 shp (tr) 24k	Torpedoed Eastern Med by *U331*, 25/11/1941
		Queen Elizabeth Class Battleship		8 - 15", 14 - 6", 2 - 3", 4 - 3pdr, 4 - 21"TT	
425	Ormonde	Orient S. N. Co.	21/10/13 - 10/2/17 - 27/10/17	580'5" x 66'7" x 40'5" x 14,853gt Turbines 17,000 shp	Scrapped Dalmuir 4/12/1952
426	Milne	Admiralty	17/2/14 - 5/10/14 - 7/12/14	273'4" x 26'7" x 16'3" x 860disp. Turbines (BC) 25,000 shp 34k	Scrapped Germany 1921
		M Class Destroyer		3 - 4", 2 - 1pdr, 4 - 21"TT	
427	Moorsom	Admiralty	27/2/14 - 20/12/14 - 17/2/15	273'4" x 26'7" x 16'3" x 860disp. Turbines (BC) 25,000 shp 34k	Scrapped Germany 1921
		M Class Destroyer		3 - 4", 2 - 1pdr, 4 - 21"TT	
428	Morris	Admiralty	26/3/14 - 19/11/14 - 31/12/14	273'4" x 26'7" x 16'3" x 860disp. Turbines (BC) 25,000 shp 34k	Scrapped Germany 1921
		M Class Destroyer		3 - 4", 2 - 1pdr, 4 - 21"TT	
429	Medea	Admiralty	6/4/14 - 30/1/15 - 22/6/15	273'4" x 26'7" x 16'3" x 860disp. Turbines (BC) 25,000 shp 32k	Scrapped by Ward, Milford 9/5/1921
	(ex *Kriti*)	Medea Class Destroyer		3 - 4", 4 - 21"TT	
430	Medusa	Admiralty	6/4/14 - 27/3/15 - 1/7/15	273'4" x 26'7" x 16'3" x 860disp. Turbines (BC) 25,000 shp 32k	Sunk in collision with *Laverick*, North Sea
	(ex *Lesvos*)	Medea Class Destroyer		3 - 4", 4 - 21"TT	
431	Pegasus	Admiralty	21/5/14 - 9/6/17 - 17/8/17	332' x 43' x 26'6" x 3,070disp. Turbines (BC) 9,500 shp	Scrapped Morecambe 8/1931
	ex *Stockholm*	Seaplane Carrier		2 - 3", 2 - 12pdr, 9 aircraft	
432	Platypus	Admiralty (RAN)	14/10/14 - 28/10/16 - 30/3/17	325' x 44' x 15'8" x 3,455disp. Triple expansion 3,500 ihp 15.5k	Scrapped Japan 1958
	Penguin, Platypus	Submarine Depot Ship			
433	Mons	Admiralty	30/9/14 - 1/5/15 - 14/7/15	273'8" x 26'9" x 16'3" x 860disp. Turbines (BC) 25,000 shp 34k	Scrapped Germany 1921
		Repeat M Class Destroyer		3 - 4", 1 - 2pdr, 4 - 21"TT	
434	Marne	Admiralty	30/9/14 - 29/5/15 - 27/9/15	273'8" x 26'9" x 16'3" x 860disp. Turbines (BC) 25,000 shp 34k	Scrapped Germany 1921
		Repeat M Class Destroyer		3 - 4", 1 - 2pdr, 4 - 21"TT	
435	Canterbury	Admiralty	14/10/14 - 21/12/15 - 9/5/16	446' x 41'6" x 16'3" x 3,750disp. Turbines 40,000 shp 29k	Scrapped Metal Industries Rosyth 15/10/1934
		Cambrian Class Cruiser		2 - 6", 8 - 4", 4 - 3pdr, 1 - 13pdr, 2 - 21"TT	
436	E35	Admiralty	7/12/14 - 20/5/16 - 14/7/16	182'6" x 22'7" x 15' x 807disp. Diesels/elec.1,600 hp/840 hp 15k/9k	Scrapped Ellis & Co Newcastle 6/9/1922
		E Class Submarine		5 - 18"TT, 1 - 12pdr.	
437	E36	Admiralty	7/1/15 - 16/9/16 - 16/11/16	182'6" x 22'7" x 15' x 807disp. Diesels/elec.1,600 hp/840 hp 15k/9k	Lost in collision North Sea 19/1/1917
		E Class Submarine		5 - 18"TT, 1 - 12pdr.	
438	E50	Admiralty	29/6/15 - 13/11/16 - 23/1/17	182'6" x 22'7" x 15' x 807disp. Diesels/elec.1,600hp/840hp 15k/9k	Lost North Sea 31/1/1918
		E Class Submarine		5 - 18"TT, 1 - 12pdr.	
439	Mameluke	Admiralty	23/12/14 - 14/8/15 - 30/10/15	273'8" x 26'9" x 16'3" x 860disp. Turbines (BC) 25,000shp 34k	Sold Cohen. Scrapped Germany 22/9/1921
		Repeat M Class Destroyer		3 - 4", 1 - 2pdr, 4 - 21"TT	
440	Ossory	Admiralty	23/12/14 - 9/10/15 - 4/12/15	273'8" x 26'9" x 16'3" x 860disp. Turbines (BC) 25,000shp 34k	Scrapped Germany 1921
		Repeat M Class Destroyer		3 - 4", 1 - 2pdr, 4 - 21"TT	
441		Admiralty	Engines for destroyer **Noble** building by Alexander Stephen. Turbines (BC) 25,000shp 34k		
442		Admiralty	Engines for destroyer **Nomad** building by Alexander Stephen. Turbines (BC) 25,000shp 34k		
443	Repulse	Admiralty	25/1/15 - 8/1/16 - 14/8/16	794' x 90' x 40' 10" x 30,835disp. Turbines (BC) 119,025shp 31.72k (t)	Sunk off Malaya 10/12/1941
		Renown Class Battlecruiser		6 - 15", 17 - 4", 2 - 3", 4 - 3pdr, 2 - 21"TT	
444	Napier	Admiralty	6/7/15 - 27/11/15 - 22/1/16	273'8" x 26'9" x 16'3" x 860disp. Turbines (BC) 25,000shp 34k	Sold Slough TC. Scrapped Germany 8/11/1921
		Repeat M Class Destroyer		3 - 4", 1 - 2pdr, 4 - 21"TT	
445	Narbrough	Admiralty	13/7/15 - 2/3/16 - 29/4/16	273'8" x 26'9" x 16'3" x 860disp. Turbines (BC) 25,000shp 34k	Wrecked off Orkney Islands 12/1/1918
		Repeat M Class Destroyer		3 - 4", 1 - 2pdr, 4 - 21"TT	
446		Admiralty	Half set of turbine machinery for battlecruiser **Furious** building by Armstrong Whitworth to order of		Scrapped Arnott Young, Dalmuir 15/3/1948
			Wallsend Slipway & Engineering Co. Ltd. (BC) 90,000 shp. 31.5k		
447	Penn	Admiralty	9/6/15 - 8/4/16 - 31/5/16	273'8" x 26'9" x 16'3" x 860disp. Turbines (BC) 25,000shp 34k	Scrapped W Burden 1921
		Repeat M Class Destroyer		3 - 4", 1 - 2pdr, 4 - 21"TT	
448	Peregrine	Admiralty	9/6/15 - 29/5/16 - 10/7/16	273'8" x 26'9" x 16'3" x 860disp. Turbines (BC) 25,000shp 34k	Scrapped Cashmore, Newport 5/11/1921
		Repeat M Class Destroyer		3 - 4", 1 - 2pdr, 4 - 21"TT	
449	Romola	Admiralty	25/8/15 - 14/5/16 - 17/8/16	275' x 26'9" x 16'3" x 975disp. Turbines (BC) 27,000shp 36k	Scrapped Troon 1930
		R Class Destroyer		3 - 4", 1 - 2pdr, 4 - 21"TT	
450	Rowena	Admiralty	25/8/15 - 1/7/16 - 29/9/16	275' x 26'9" x 16'3" x 975disp. Turbines (BC) 27,000shp 36k	Scrapped Ward, Milford Haven 1937
		R Class Destroyer		3 - 4", 1 - 2pdr, 4 - 21"TT	
451	Restless	Admiralty	22/9/15 - 12/8/16 - 21/10/16	275' x 26'9" x 16'3" x 975disp. Turbines(BC) 27,000shp 36k	Scrapped Ward, Briton Ferry 11/1936
		R Class Destroyer		3 - 4", 1 - 2pdr, 4 - 21"TT	
452	Rigorous	Admiralty	22/9/15 - 30/9/16 - 27/11/16	275' x 26'9" x 16'3" x 975disp. Turbines (BC) 27,000shp 36k	Scrapped Cashmore, Newport 5/11/1926
		R Class Destroyer		3 - 4", 1 - 2pdr, 4 - 21"TT	
453		Admiralty	Geared turbines (BC) for K Class **K1** submarine building at Portsmouth Dyd. 10,500shp		
454		Admiralty	Geared turbines (BC) for K Class **K2** submarine building at Portsmouth Dyd. 10,500shp		
455	Simoom	Admiralty	23/5/16 - 30/10/16 - 22/12/16	275' x 26'9" x 16'3" x 975disp. Turbines (BC) 27,000shp 36k	Sunk North Sea 23/1/1917
		R Class Destroyer		3 - 4", 1 - 2pdr, 4 - 21"TT	

No	Name	Owner	Keel - Launch - Completion	Basic Particulars	Fate
456	**Windsor Castle**	Union Castle Mail S. S. Co	4/6/19 - 9/3/21 - 10/3/22	630' x 72'3" x 41'5" x 19,600gt Geared turbines 14,500shp 18k	Lost 23/3/1943
457	**Tarpon**	Admiralty R Class Destroyer	12/4/16 - 10/3/17 - 26/4/17	276' x 26'9" x 16'3" x 900disp. Turbines (BC) 27,000shp 3 - 4", 1 - 2pdr, 4 - 21"TT	Scrapped Cashmore, Newport 8/1927
458	**Telemachus**	Admiralty R Class Destroyer	12/4/16 - 21/4/17 - 16/6/17	276' x 26'9" x 16'3" x 900disp. Turbines (BC) 27,000shp 3 - 4", 1 - 2pdr, 4 - 21"TT	Scrapped Hughes Bolckow, Blyth 8/1927
459	**Ceres**	Admiralty Cruiser Class cruiser	26/4/16 - 24/3/17 - 15/6/17	450' x 43'6" x 24' 9" x 4,190disp. Turbines (BC) 39,425shp 29.1k 5 - 6", 2 - 3", 4 - 3pdr, 8 - 21"TT	Scrapped Hughes Bolckow, Blyth 12/7/1946
460	**Hood**	Admiralty Battlecruiser	1/9/16 -22/8/18 - 15/5/20c	860' 7" x 104' 2" x 40' 10" 46,680disp. Geared turbines (BC) 151,280shp 32.07k(t) 8 x 15", 12 x 5.5", 4 x 4", 6 x 21"TT	Sunk Denmark Strait 24/5/1941
461	**Skate**	Admiralty R Class Destroyer	12/1/16 - 11/1/17 - 19/2/17	275' x 26'9" x 16'3" x 975disp. Turbines (BC) 27,000shp 36k 3 - 4", 1 - 2pdr, 4 - 21"TT	Scrapped Newport 1947
462	**Vanoc**	Admiralty V Class Destroyer	20/9/16 - 14/6/17 - 15/8/17	312' x 29'6" x 18' 3" x 1,490disp. Geared turbines (BC) 27,000shp 34k 4 - 4", 1 - 3", 4 - 21"TT	Lost 1946 en route to shipbreakers
463	**Vanquisher**	Admiralty V Class Destroyer	29/9/16 - 18/8/17 - 2/10/17	312' x 29'6" x 18' 3" x 1,490disp. Geared turbines (BC) 27,000shp 34k 4 - 4", 1 - 3", 4 - 21"TT	Scrapped Charlestown 1948
464	**Montcalm** *Wolfe*	Canadian Pacific Rly	10/1/19 - 3/7/20 - 15/12/21	575' x 70'2" x 43'3" x 16,418gt Geared turbines 14,000 shp 17.5k	Scrapped Faslane November 1952
465	**Montclare**	Canadian Pacific Rly	17/9/19 - 17/12/21 - 2/8/22	575' x 70'6" x 43'3" x 16,314gt Geared turbines 14,000 shp 17k	Scrapped Inverkeithing 1958
466	**Wakeful**	Admiralty W Class Destroyer	17/1/17 - 6/10/17 - 16/11/17	312' x 29'6" x 18' 3" x 1,490disp. Geared turbines (BC) 27,000shp 34k	Sunk off Dunkirk 30/5/1940
467	**Watchman**	Admiralty W Class Destroyer	17/1/17 - 1/12/17 - 26/1/18	312' x 29'6" x 18' 3" x 1,490disp. Geared turbines (BC) 27,000shp 34k	Scrapped Inverkeithing 1945
468	**War Thistle** *Emilie D*	Ship Controller	2/3/17 - 1/9/17 - 9/10/17	412' x 52'2" x 31' x 5,152gt Triple expansion 2,500ihp	Wrecked near Finisterre 8/10/1927
469	**War Hermit** *Anatina, Mindanao*	Anglo Saxon Petroleum	12/3/17 - 28/3/18 - 29/4/18	412' x 52'3" x 31' x 5,256gt Triple expansion 2,500ihp (engine by Fullerton Hodgart & Barclay, Paisley)	Sunk Japanese aircraft Mindoro Island 10/2/1942
470	**War Rider** *Fort de Troyon, Eridano, Al Kuwait, Spetsai Sailor*	Chargeurs Reunis	7/9/17 - 6/9/18 - ?/1/19	412' x 52'4" x 31' x 5,269t Triple expansion 2,500ihp	Sunk off Aden after springing leak 11/10/58
471	**War Crane** *Bodnant*	African S.S. Co.	8/4/18 - 3/6/19 - 2/7/19	412' x 52'3" x 31' x 5,258t Triple expansion 2,500ihp	Sunk after collision south of Iceland 30/12/40
472	**Simoom**	Admiralty S Class Destroyer	2/7/17 - 26/1/18 - 12/3/18	276' x 26'9" x 16' 3" x 1,075disp. Geared turbines (BC) 27,000shp 36k 3 - 4", 1 - 2pdr, 4 - 21"TT	Scrapped Metal Industries, Charlestown 2/31
473	**Scimitar**	Admiralty S Class Destroyer	30/5/17 - 27/2/18 - 29/4/18	276' x 26'9" x 16' 3" x 1,075disp. Geared turbines (BC) 27,000shp 36k 3 - 4", 1 - 2pdr, 4 - 21"TT	Scrapped Ward, Briton Ferry 1947
474	**Scotsman**	Admiralty S Class Destroyer	10/12/17 - 30/3/18 - 21/5/18	276' x 26'9" x 16' 3" x 1,075disp. Geared turbines (BC) 27,000shp 36k 3 - 4", 1 - 2pdr, 4 - 21"TT	Scrapped Ward, Briton Ferry 1937
475	**Scout**	Admiralty S Class Destroyer	25/10/17 - 27/4/18 - 15/6/18	276' x 26'9" x 16' 3" x 1,075disp. Geared turbines (BC) 27,000shp 36k 3 - 4", 1 - 2pdr, 4 - 21"TT	Scrapped Ward, Briton Ferry 1946
476	**Scythe**	Admiralty S Class Destroyer	4/1/18 - 25/5/18 - 8/7/18	276' x 26'9" x 16' 3" x 1,075disp. Geared turbines (BC) 27,000shp 36k 3 - 4", 1 - 2pdr, 4 - 21"TT	Scrapped Newport 1931
477	**Seabear**	Admiralty S Class Destroyer	13/12/17 - 6/7/18 - 7/9/18	276' x 26'9" x 16' 3" x 1,075disp. Geared turbines (BC) 27,000shp 36k 3 - 4", 1 - 2pdr, 4 - 21"TT	Scrapped, Ward (Grays) 2/31
478	**Seafire**	Admiralty S Class Destroyer	27/2/18 - 10/8/18 - 24/10/18	276' x 26'9" x 16' 3" x 1,075disp. Geared turbines (BC) 27,000shp 36k 3 - 4", 1 - 2pdr, 4 - 21"TT	Scrapped, Ward, Inverkeithing 7/36
479	**Searcher**	Admiralty S Class Destroyer	30/3/18 - 11/9/18 - 25/11/18	276' x 26'9" x 16' 3" x 1,075disp. Geared turbines (BC) 27,000shp 36k 3 - 4", 1 - 2pdr, 4 - 21"TT	Scrapped, Ward, Barrow 3/38
480	**Seawolf**	Admiralty S Class Destroyer	30/4/18 - 2/11/18 - 28/1/19	276' x 26'9" x 16' 3" x 1,075disp. Geared turbines (BC) 27,000shp 36k 3 - 4", 1 - 2pdr, 4 - 21"TT	Scrapped, Newport 1930 following collision
481		Admiralty		Machinery for destroyer **Sesame** building at Wm Denny. Geared turbines (BC) 27,000shp 36k	
482	**Venomous** (ex *Venom*)	Admiralty Modified W Class Destroyer	31/5/18 - 21/12/18 - 6/19	312' x 29'6" x 18' 3" x 1,508disp. Geared turbines (BC) 27,000shp 34k 4 - 4.7", 1 - 3" or 2 - 2pdr, 6 - 21"TT	Scrapped, Charlestown 1946
483	**Verity**	Admiralty Modified W Class Destroyer	17/5/18 - 19/3/19 - 17/9/19	312' x 29'6" x 18' 3" x 1,508disp. Geared turbines (BC) 27,000shp 34k 4 - 4.7", 1 - 3" or 2 - 2pdr, 6 - 21"TT	Scrapped, Newport 1947
484	**Enterprise**	Admiralty Emerald Class Cruiser	28/6/18 - 23/12/19 - 9/4/20	570' x 54'6" x 16'6" x 7,558disp. Geared turbines (BC) 80,000shp 33k (After launch completed at Devonport) 7 - 6", 5 - 4", 4 - 3pdr, 3 -2pdr, 12 - 21"TT	Scrapped, Newport 1946
485	**Veteran**	Admiralty Modified W Class Destroyer	30/8/18 - 26/4/19 - 12/11/19	312' x 29'6" x 18' 3" x 1,508disp. Turbines 27,000shp 34k 4 - 4.7", 1 - 3" or 2 - 2pdr, 6 - 21"TT	Sunk by *U404* 26/9/42
486	**Vigo**	Admiralty Modified W Class Destroyer	CANCELLED	312' x 29'6" x 18' 3" x 1,508disp. Turbines 27,000shp 34k 4 - 4.7", 1 - 3" or 2 - 2pdr, 6 - 21"TT	
487	**Wistful** (ex *Vigorous*)	Admiralty Modified W Class Destroyer	CANCELLED	312' x 29'6" x 18' 3" x 1,500disp. Turbines 27,000shp 34k 4 - 4.7", 1 - 3" or 2 - 2pdr, 6 - 21"TT	
488	**Virulent**	Admiralty Modified W Class Destroyer	CANCELLED	312' x 29'6" x 18' 3" x 1,500disp. Turbines 27,000shp 34k 4 - 4.7", 1 - 3" or 2 - 2pdr, 6 - 21"TT	
489	**Volage**	Admiralty Modified W Class Destroyer	CANCELLED	312' x 29'6" x 18' 3" x 1,500disp. Turbines 27,000shp 34k 4 - 4.7", 1 - 3" or 2 - 2pdr, 6 - 21"TT	
490	**Volcano**	Admiralty Modified W Class Destroyer	CANCELLED	312' x 29'6" x 18' 3" x 1,500disp. Turbines 27,000shp 34k 4 - 4.7", 1 - 3" or 2 - 2pdr, 6 - 21"TT	
491	**Bata** *Tower Abbey, Willandra, Utide Maru*	Elder Dempster Lines	19/12/18 - 10/9/19 - 14/10/19	412' x 52'3" x 31' x 5,100gt Triple expansion 2,500ihp (by H&W)	Sunk by submarine USS *Sargo* 29/2/1944

INDEX

A

Acasta 23
Achates 23
Admiralty, The 9, 13, 15, 40, 47, 70, 168
Almirante Cochrane 15
Anchor Line 40
Antrim 19
Antwerp 15, 178
Aquitania 7, 8, 17, 21, 22, 24, 28, 30, 33, 36, 37, 41, 42, 45, 47
Argyll and Southern Highlanders, The 58
Armstrong Whitworth & Co Ltd 7, 9, 87
Arran 180
Arrol, Sir William & Co Ltd 24, 42, 49
Askold (Glory IV) 57, 109
Australia 8, 21, 26, 28
Australian Imperial Force 146
Aydon 69

B

Babcock & Wilcox, Renfrew 117
Barclay Curle & Co Ltd 149
Barham 8, 11, 14, 34, 49, 50, 54, 58, 61, 62, 65, 66, 69, 72, 75, 76, 79, 80, 82, 83, 85, 130
Barley, Captain George 175
Barr & Stroud 21
Barrosa 8
Barrow in Furness 7, 69, 97
Bassett Lowke 166
Bata 15
Battle of Jutland 13
Battle of Tsushima 21
Beardmore William & Co Ltd 7, 9, 23, 56, 101, 127
Bell, (Sir) Thomas 10, 11, 45, 183
Bermuda 8
Bethlehem Steel Corporation 80
Birkenhead 7, 95
Black Sea, The 95
Bordeaux 52
Brisk 20
British Imperial War Cabinet 164
Brown-Curtis turbines 9, 20, 21, 111, 57, 62, 87, 88, 153, 177
Bruge 15

C

Cammell Laird & Co Ltd 7, 40, 95
Campania 40
Canada 15
Canadian Pacific Railways 15, 149, 182
Canadian Pacific Steamships 27
Canterbury 88, 95, 96, 97, 98
Carinthia 8
Carmania 9
Caronia 8
Castor 95
Ceres 132, 136, 138, 140, 166
Chadburn's (engine telegraph) 41
Chantiers et Ateliers de la Gironde 52
Charles Cammell 7
Charles Curtis 9
Chatham, HM Dockyard 13
Churchill, Winston 79
City of New York 18
Clyde Navigation Trust, The 6
Clydebank Battlecruisers 7, 8
Clydebank Shipbuilding & Engineering Co Ltd 7
Colville, David, & Co Ltd 72
Controlled Establishment 10
Controller of Shipping, The 13, 145
Controller, The 13
Coventry Ordnance Works 7
Cowans Sheldon 42
Cunard Co 7, 47

D

Denny, William & Co Ltd, Dumbarton 95
Derby, The Countess of 33
Destroyer Flotilla, 11th 95
Devonport, HM Dockyard 177
Director of Naval Construction (DNC) 13
Dreadnought 7
Duchess of Rothesay 50
Duke of York 8
Dunbartonshire Volunteers, The 58
Duncan, Charles MP 80
Dunkirk 129

E

E35 13, 91, 100, 101, 102, 103, 105, 106
E50 119
Eagle 15
Elder Dempster 15
Elderslie Dockyard 136
Elswick 97
Elswick Ordnance Works 80
Emerald 177
Empress of Russia 27
Enterprise 15, 177
Erebus 91

F

Fairfield Shipbuilding & Engineering Co Ltd 7, 9, 13, 27, 70, 93, 117, 149
Federal Steam Navigation Co 22
First World War 7, 8, 9, 10, 23, 49
Firth of Clyde 65, 180
Firth of Forth 40
Fisher, Lady 183
Fisher, Lord 11, 13, 79
Flying Elf 56
Flying Scotsman 52, 160
Flying Swallow 52
Flying Wizard 23
Fortune 8
France 52
Furious 15, 87

G

Gallipoli 79, 95
Gareloch 106
General Electric Co, Schenectady 9
Govan 7, 65, 93, 120, 149
Grand Fleet, The 13
Great Eastern Railway Co 15, 130, 178

H

Hamburg America Line 33
Hamilton, William, & Co Ltd 61
Harland & Wolff Ltd 91, 95, 157
Harwich Force, The 120
High Seas Fleet 11
Hood 7, 8, 13, 15, 120, 127, 148, 152, 157, 165, 170, 171, 174, 178, 179, 180
Hugh McLean & Co 45

I

Imperatitsa Mariya 57
Imperator Aleksandr III 15, 57, 109, 111
Imperator Class 33
Inflexible 7

J

Jutland, Battle of 95

K

K1 15, 153
K2 15, 153
K7 151
King George V, HRH 50
Kriti (later Medea) 70

L

Lapland 157
Lascelles, Hon Mrs Edward 88
Lesvos (later Medusa) 70
Lusitania 7, 8

M

M4 (later Raglan) 80
Mameluke 84
Meadowside Quay 125
Medea 54, 76, 79
Medusa 54, 79
Milne 54, 56, 57
Ministry of Munitions, The 134
Mirrlees Watson & Co Ltd 134
Missanabie 149
Montcalm 15, 182, 183
Moon 80
Moorsom 13, 54, 64
Morris 54
Motherwell 72
Munitions of War Act 9
Munitions, Ministry of 10

N

Napier 13
National Records of Scotland 9
New Zealand 26
Newshot Island 28
Nikolaev 111
Noble 15
Nomad 15

O

Official Secrets Act 8
Orient Steam Navigation Co 129
Ormonde 15, 125, 127, 129, 132, 145, 146, 166

P

Palmers, Shipbuilding Co Ltd 9, 13
Parsons (turbines) 9
Pegasus 15, 141, 142, 172
Platypus 119, 127, 136
Port Glasgow 61
Portsmouth, HM Dockyard 153
Prince Rupert 61, 76, 76, 77

Q

QE2 8
Queen Alexandria 95
Queen Mary, RMS 8

R

Ramillies 8, 9
Red Cross Society 95
Red Star Line 157
Renown 9, 13, 117
Repulse 7, 8, 9, 13, 15, 70, 72, 79, 87, 91, 93, 95, 97, 102, 111, 112, 117, 129
Richborough, Kent 149
River Cart 7

Romola 91, 97, 114, 115
Rothesay Dock 172
Rowena 91, 114
Royal Australian Navy 136
Royal Mail Line 95, 132
Royal Oak 40

S

Salamis 80
Scimitar 151, 158
Scotsman 13, 151, 162
Scotstoun 8
Scout 162
Scythe 13
Scythe 171
Seabear 168, 172
Seafire 15, 174
Searcher 15, 168
Seawolf 14, 168
Second World War 8
Sesame 13, 15
Ship Experiment Tank, Clydebank 20
Simoom 120, 154
Smutts, Lieutenant General Jan 164
Southampton 8
St Margaret of Scotland (*Balantia*) 95
Stockholm (HMS *Pegasus*) 15, 130
Swindon 11

T

Tarpon 13, 129
Telemachus 13, 129, 132
Thomson, James and George 7, 8
Tiger 7, 8, 10, 11, 14, 42, 50, 55, 130
Titanic 33
Togo, Admiral 21
Train Ferry No 3 (later HMS *Daffodil*) 149
Tsushima, Battle of 109
Turbine Steamers Ltd 95
Tyne, River 149

U

UB78 95
United States 9
Upper Clyde Shipbuilders Ltd 9

V

Valiant 93
Vanoc 144
Vanquisher 166
Venom 15
Venomous 168
Verity 15, 168
Verity's Ltd 103
Veteran 15, 178, 179
Vickers Son & Maxim Ltd 7, 13, 61, 69
Victorious 61

Vigo 13, 15
Virulent 13
Volage 13
Volcano 13
Vulkan AG, Hamburg 80

W

Wakeful 147
Wallsend Slipway 87
War Crane 14
War Hermit 15, 145, 155, 160
War Office, The 129
War Rider 15, 172
War Thistle 15, 145, 166
Weston Electrical Equipment Co 103
Whipp & Bourne 103
Wiltshire 22
Wistful 13
Wolhandel 111
Women dilutees 122, 123

Y

Yarrow (boilers) 134

1914

Aquitania

1915

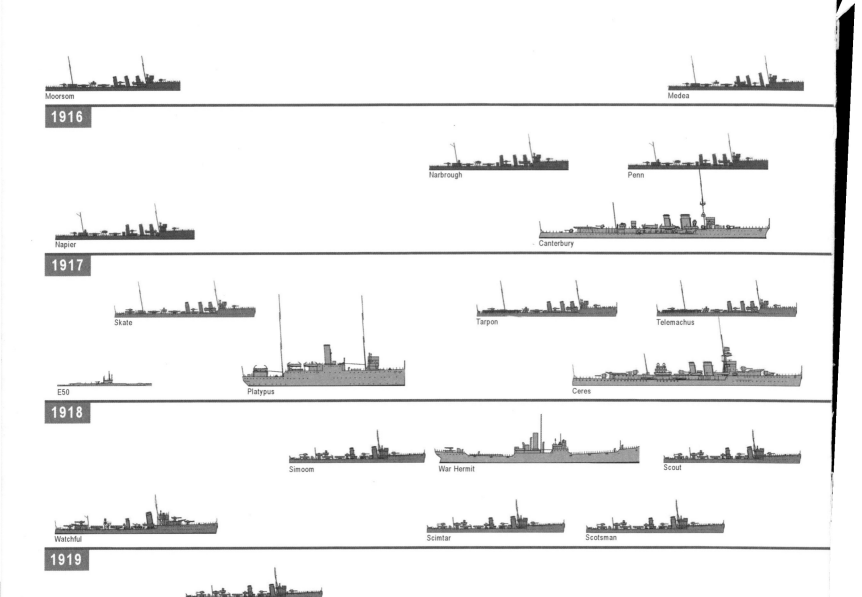

Moorsom

Medea

1916

Narbrough

Penn

Napier

Canterbury

1917

Skate

Tarpon

Telemachus

E50

Platypus

Ceres

1918

Simoom

War Hermit

Scout

Watchful

Scimtar

Scotsman

1919

Seawolf

War Rider